How We Learn to Read

Books by Seymour W. Itzkoff

The Evolution of Human Intelligence
An Argument in Series

This is where it all begins

HOW WE LEARN TO READ

Seymour W. Itzkoff

Smith College

Paideia Publishers
Ashfield, Massachusetts

Published in the United States by
Paideia Publishers
P.O. Box 343,
Ashfield, Massachusetts 01330

Library of Congress Cataloging in Publication Data

Itzkoff, Seymour W.
    How we learn to read.

    Bibliography: p.
    Includes index.
    1. Reading. 2. Reading readiness. I. Title
LB1050.I89   1986   372.4   85-29879
ISBN 0-913993-04-2
ISBN 0-913993-05-0 (pbk.)

To my students in

"THE READING PROCESS"

Acknowledgments

A teacher who writes a book based on a course developed and taught over many years cannot easily assign his debt to any one group of students. It was their puzzlement, papers, questions that gradually forced me to think through the fascinating issues that psycholinguistic theory had dredged up and placed before educators in general and trainers of teachers in particular.

Well, here it is, still unfinished, a set of ideas that will require further shaping and amplification. Perhaps more questions and controversies will lead me once more to the drawing board. I hope so.

To Helen Kihmm, for her work in typing, editorial fine-tuning, and on the index, and to Jane Lewin, for her bibliographical assistance, many thanks. Smith College deserves an ongoing nod for providing me the students to teach, the assistants to help with the manuscript, and all the services that make scholarly work possible.

Patricia Stroman of Paideia Publishers guided the manuscript to publication with her usual patient tenacity, although I do think that this time she was a bit more resigned to my foibles than usual. At any rate, the responsibilities are mine. I did want to set this one asail upon the waters. Perhaps it will create a few waves.

Contents

Illustrations

Frontispiece: This is where it all begins

PART I

What Is Reading?

1

Introduction:
Reconciliation
in Reading

T HE READING WAR still goes on. If it is not as before a
full-scale conflagration with its public divisions and
deeply-scarred partisans, the guerrilla encounters and the occasional firefights continue to tell us that the salve of national
reform has yet to do its work. Why are we still battling over
the proper reading method: phonics vs. sight/whole-word
reading?

Since the early 1970's, a revolution has occurred in our
understanding of language acquisition and reading. The discipline of psycholinguistics has reshaped our knowledge of the
relationship of the brain and language. In the process, we
now have a much clearer understanding of what happens
when we read fluently. While we have seen the publication

and wide dissemination of one important book on the psycholinguistics reading process, *Understanding Reading*, 1971, by Frank Smith, the application of these ideas has not found its way into our classrooms nor into the understanding of teachers and parents.

This is regrettable, because there has been an impact here on the old debate between phonics teaching and look-say (sight/whole-word). If we follow the literature as represented in the most important scholarly journal in reading, *The Reading Research Quarterly*, from about 1971 on, we are aware that the old divisions have faded. Unfortunately, the practical application of this new knowledge has yet to come to the fore. The skirmishing as to how we should teach reading continues.

Since 1972, I have been teaching a course at Smith College entitled "The Reading Process." While I awaited the sequel to Frank Smith's book—which I hoped to be an explanation of the acquisition of reading competency and its application in the classroom—I did my own homework, to help my students see the meaning of this psycholinguistics revolution.

However, I waited in vain. For, as we crossed into the 1980's, it became clear from the *Quarterly* and other educational journals that the opportunity had been allowed to pass. Issues such as readability, vocabulary and syntactic (sentence structure) difficulties were becoming the focus of research. The gradual decline of reading levels in our nation was being answered in the profession by an acquiescence that concerned itself with making reading "easy," as if such simplifications in text materials could really obviate the need to read difficult and challenging materials outside of school in a more competitive intellectual and technological world.

Further, the actual textbooks for future teachers of reading in the schools, instead of attempting to show the relationship of phonics and whole-word (look-say) instruction, merely added them in a mostly helter-skelter pot-pourri of skills to which the teacher should expose children as part of the pedagogical repertoire. The actual reading text series that children in schools learned from also were suffused by this touch-all-bases, safety-net approach. No publisher wanted to be labeled phonics-oriented nor would they want the political taint that attached to the progressivist whole-word approach of the thirties and forties.

How We Learn to Read is an attempt to damp the fires of contention by offering an ecumenical theoretical and practical approach. I do not have any ideological axe to grind. Rather, presented here is a rich scientific literature on psycholinguistics and reading (unfortunately not to have reached the public) that has met the test of almost two decades of critical study. This work I hope will translate this knowledge into a form that will be systematic as well as understandable.

Before summarizing the main arguments in the book as I will develop them, let me first state that the overriding theme that will interest students of reading, teachers, and parents is that there is room in a modern scientific concept of reading for both an aspect of phonics teaching as well as the general whole-word/sight approach. The reader of this book will, however, have to pay careful attention to the special significance and character of both approaches, for they are laid out as part of the developmental process of how the human being learns to read in an alphabetic language.

The latter qualification is important, because for languages such as Chinese, which are "logographic" in the sense that the written characters do not necessarily have a set phonemic value, the problems commonly associated with learning to read in English will not necessarily apply. However, I do believe that for other, alphabetic, languages, even those that contain far fewer exceptions in the correlation of letters with sounds, the theory here to be set forth about reading and its pedagogical implications will hold.

The first section of the book puts the problem of learning to read in an historical perspective. To understand better what human purpose reading serves, we ought to look back to the origins of literacy, then to the educational challenge of teaching this esoteric skill to the young. The debates that have since arisen are part of the natural frictions that accompany a growing and learning process. There is something powerful in an understanding of causes in that it helps us predict consequences. With the new knowledge that we have attained about the nature of human language and its written abstract embodiment, we will be able to clear out the obfuscation, conflict, cant, and hysteria that have bogged us down.

The second part of the book attempts to do just this, by unfolding a developmental sequence in the context of schooling for the process of learning to read. Here I propose a three-phase structure in the acquisition of reading competency. The first has to do with readiness, the gradual introduction of the child to written patterns, awareness that letter symbols stand generally for certain common and easily distinguishable sounds: "a" for "apple," "c" for "candy," "m" for "mama," "E" for "Edith," etc. The reading readiness stage wherein we evaluate the child's evolving discriminatory powers prepares the ground for what is called "mediated reading."

In this stage, phonics instruction may be useful. There is a point in the child's neurological development—a median age of 6.5 years has been traditional—when the child is able to look at words, recognize their spatial/visual patterns, and correlate these patterns with their spoken equivalents. Children who can break this so-called "featural code" are able to bypass tedious instruction in the relationship of letters to sounds and go quickly, with a minimum of phonic clues, to the reading of words, sentences, and paragraphs in ever more efficient visual gulps.

However, a large percentage of youngsters needs more help. For various reasons these youngsters need to be guided to make the slow step-like decoding of the visual symbols to their sound-spoken equivalents before they can understand the words. Only gradually as we carefully clue children into this magical world of "language through vision" and by the use of a special kind of phonics instruction will reading fluency become part of their repertoire of learning skills.

Phonics teaching where required should be thought of only as a stage on the way toward rapid featural encoding of the visual word patterns directly to meaning and comprehension. Phonics ought never become an instructional end in itself in the reading process. It is much too slow and befuddling ever to lead to ease and enjoyment of reading for understanding and appreciation.

Thus we introduce fluent reading, which is neither phonics nor whole-word identification. If it seems closer to the latter, it is only because as part of the fluent reading process, we do identify words as wholes, but so do we rapidly move on to sentences, and then, with particularly good readers, to the comprehension of entire paragraphs. The key here is not the word as a whole, but those shorthand visual features that the neurologically matured youngsters can distill from their rapidly moving visual reading gulps into meaningful units, whether words, sentences, or paragraphs.

From this understanding as to how children learn to read, some with ease, others with difficulty, a pattern of knowledge has emerged that has illuminated a wide area of research dealing with reading and writing. Foremost is the realization that there is an aspect of reading as a skill that cannot be merged into general intelligence. Reading, like math, music, art, and a myriad of abilities that cannot clearly be coordinated with intelligence, is often an independent variable. Thus it can be understood as a disability without impugning the intellectual capacity of an individual.

There are literally millions of truly learning-disabled children, many of them reading-handicapped (dyslectic) who are otherwise highly intelligent. (There is a view that proposes that they are above-average in intelligence as a group.) The existence and analysis of such handicaps have led us to postulate what I here call the reading or *integrational* dimension of learning to read. An appendix is included to explain the integrational factor in more detail. The integrational process explains the variability of children of all dimensions of intelligence to learn to read, and through various modalities—visual, auditory, even tactile. It helps make us realize that reading-disabled children are different from slow learners, and that indeed poor readers can sometimes be math whizzes or even potential Leonardo da Vincis.

The final section of *How We Learn to Read* places the developmental picture within a pedagogical frame. How do we best teach reading? One of the byproducts of the ongoing debate over the nature of reading has been the development of a number of different reading textbook series that served to make concrete the particular philosophy of reading that it expressed.

What I do in this section on reading series approaches is to show how we have fallen into error and thus short-changed our young learners. In the process we have transformed into ideological politics what ought to be an open-minded search for effective educational tools that reflect our experience. We ought not do as the Soviets once did, destroy their agriculture for the sake of dogma. Unlike agriculture, where we often have a new beginning in the next year, a child lives on for several generations. In the process, a nation can fall.

My goal in this final section is more tentative, more one of clarification and practical reasonableness than scientific surety. For example, I do make a distinction between curricular and pedagogical approaches to the teaching of reading. The reading curriculum should present a consistent theoretical content orientation to the nature of the reading process and how the person acquires this skill and in what sequence.

Pedagogy or teaching method can be more flexible, often being equally adapted to various curricular content approaches in reading. Whether the teacher is group- or individually-oriented can be unaffected by the particular curricular philosophy being espoused. However, it can often be crucial. That is why it is vital that we keep things separate in our minds that have different functions: a curriculum being a subject matter of the reading process—substance; teaching method, the way to approach or convey that substance to the child, a very different kind of issue from curriculum.

In the final chapters are discussed the implications of this new knowledge about reading in the light that it throws on the nature of human individuation, the various talents of children, as well as the broader implications for society in dealing with the variable abilities in reading that we meet with in the world and now find confirmed and made intelligible by our theory. The meaning of these facts is rather somber for that eternal educational grail—universal literacy. Universal literacy probably cannot be achieved, in reality, and it probably ought not to be striven for directly as a matter of national policy.

The ability to read with depth and understanding in this era of heavy exposure to the written medium can only be inhibited by (1) negative curricular and pedagogical factors, especially the former, and (2) a family and social environment that is nonintellectual and shallow. These latter concerns are far more significant social and national issues than even the search for universal literacy. What good does it do us if, let us say, 100 percent of the people read at least on the fourth-grade level, but only twenty percent read beyond tenth grade. Would it not be better to have thirty percent at less than a fourth-grade reading level and forty percent reading beyond tenth grade?

If one important truth emerges from this study of the reading process, it is that reading itself is a specialized skill that in many ways has its own internal laws and development, apart from a human being's general intellectual development. It thus argues that in order to read well, one cannot merely hope to develop general intellectual skills apart from the special disciplines that reading and writing necessitate. In addition, it is clear that reading and writing in their depths open vast new ranges of thought and knowledge that ordinary visual and commonsense experience cannot hope to make possible for the individual.

We are not being honest about the source of our declining literacy, technology, cultural ambience, if we merely point at the school. Certainly, as the reader will note in the chapters that follow, to a large degree, systematic phonics instruction in reading over the past generation has had its destructive impact. In the days of look-say/whole-word reading, you either got it or you didn't.

More recently, phonics instruction has caught some of the incipient failures in its net. It has, however, through its tedious rule-governed approach uniformly created a generation of inhibited and slow readers, who don't really enjoy reading. At a certain stage in the child's educational development, even the most zealous phonics teachers let go and allow the child to learn to read on his/her own. At that point, outside events overwhelm the school's efforts. If these extracurricular influences—family, friends, society—are contraeducative, the school can do little.

Today we are a society of affluent spectators. The deeper pleasures of reading and writing do need work and dedication to flower. The truth is that the general sharpening of intelligence needs the practice of reading and writing, for these lead to a hundred byways of complex, abstract thought, in a wide variety of symbolic languages. The kind of mentation required here is quite different from that cultivated in front of a T.V. set or in conversation at the soda fountain with one's friends.

How We Learn To Read is intended to place in perspective the biopsychological elements involved in educating a person for reading competency. It is my hope that by putting aside those ancient internecine battles between the Hatfields/phonics and McCoys/whole-word advocates, we can get on to an examination of the larger question of educational reform.

2

Literacy

Heritage of Talent

THE TRUK ISLANDERS travel thousands of miles across the Pacific Ocean in open longboats. Invariably they debark at a precise, predetermined location. It is a tradition that they have retained since primeval times, a tradition beyond recall of memory or purpose. Without compass, astrolabe, or sextant, they make their way by an uncanny understanding of the structure of the heavens, the position of stars and constellations, the movement of planets.

What intellectual means have they developed to control and organize such experience and understanding? Certainly they do not write down the laws of navigation, for until recently they were not literate. As powerful as these intellectual skills were for their survival over the ages, are these same talents the wave of their future destiny?

They speak of the Mayan weavers of Cantrell. These women, shown a sample pattern and despite having to adapt their traditional weaving procedures to modern mechanized looms, can transform the visual pattern into the mechanical realization with rarely a first try, slip, or error. Their visual, patterned memory helps them to make the transition between folk tradition and modern industry. It does not necessarily prepare them for startling achievements in language, reading, or writing. Their world is still largely the folk ways of their ancestors. Wall Street, Madison Avenue, Harvard Square have not yet elicited a response from them.

The Eskimos, able to harpoon barely perceptible seals from their movements under the ice were able to transfer their skills to taking apart and putting together auto and airplane motors, virtually from first exposure, and largely through observation. What teaching they received for this latter skill was cursory. The visual and intellectual skills demanded to remember the order and arrangement of the parts of the motor, their interrelationships—all without elaborate manuals—seem awesome to us. They are apparently built into the Eskimos' innate talents, previously unexploited potentialities that have developed as byproducts of the demanding existence of life on the ice.

There are many and various skills all over the world, from potting and basket making among the simple folk cultures to the amazing skills of recognition and pursuit among the few remaining hunters scattered about the continents. Are these talents the wave of the future? Do we even need the proverbial mechanical abilities of an Eskimo to assemble and disassemble engines? Does the cost of supporting such talented individuals in a modern style equal the savings created by computerized assembly and disassembly of dozens of such engines?

What kinds of visual talents do we require in those operations centers where two eyes scan instrument boards and panels seemingly to coordinate complex yet fully automated procedures? If the red light flickers or the bell rings, those eyes will react and, presumably, human hands will press the alert button. One suspects that in the flow of time, machines, not humans, will watch the boards and press the buttons. New talents will be required by the human shapers of nature's enigmatic pool of ancient skills.

The world that requires reading and its associated skills and disciplines is overtaking us. It is a tidal wave. Soon on every part of our globe the ancient skills and traditions will have been pushed into the past.

What kind of skill is this bedeviling thing called reading? How does it correlate with those needed educational instrumentalities of the late twentieth century? What has caused literacy to dominate our lives? Why were so many other precious talents and patterns of existence rendered redundant for future survival? Finally, why do reading skills vary so greatly, not merely from individual to individual, but from national group to national group, geography to geography.

Important as they are, these are all background issues to the preeminent questions in our own day. If reading and literacy are so crucial to the intellectual development necessary for survival, how can we teach reading, educate the young and old to become literate so that they can utilize to the maximum their own inner abilities?

Markings, Pictures, Letters

When considered in the context of the human genus, *Homo*, whose members were probably able to communicate verbally, if rudimentarily, as long as five million years ago, written language is virtually a contemporary invention. Alexander Marshack, in his *Roots of Civilization* and other writings, has persuasively argued that the markings on bone and stone of Upper Paleolithic cave people were chronometric attempts to regularize symbolically the rhythmic periodicities of human experience, much as the English megaliths at Stonehenge, for example, seem to be lined up to catch the sun at its solstice turning points (June 21, December 21) along the respective horizons. Marshack thinks that the ancient Cro-Magnons 25,000 years ago notated such events as lunar periodicity, menstrual and pregnancy rhythms, the migration of animals, the seasons much as the hunter notches the stock of his gun, to remind him of the events, the days, and to see with his own eyes the total pattern, in one glance, that passed slowly before his senses over the weeks and months. It became a "story" for the mind.

These mysterious and enigmatic jottings were lost in time. The ice retreated and the European and west Asian cave civilizations broke up; the neothermal period had begun. As the herds went north to the fir forests and the tundra, many humans went south, especially into the river valleys. The skills of sculpting, hunting, and painting, which they had cultivated for over 25,000 years, much like the skills that our contemporary preliterates cultivate, were soon transformed by need into a new social pattern.

Agriculture, herding, commerce, and manufacture soon became transferred to small towns situated either in oases or alongside flowing streams. Here, along the Tigris and Euphrates rivers of our contemporary Iraq, among the talented Sumerians, literacy was born. Possibly as early as 3500 B.C., pictographs—pictures of ideas and things—were being carved into wood or stone. Later they were etched into clay. Humans were communicating to other humans out of sight and hearing.

Why then or there? The answer seems to arise from the social needs. Just as today, literacy skills dominated the workplace. The complexity of economic life in their cities began to increase. Some kind of notation was needed to organize, record, and communicate large amounts of information that the mind could hardly be expected to hold, memorize, and recall accurately. Just as the written book can give us immediately what a talented bard would take days to communi-

26

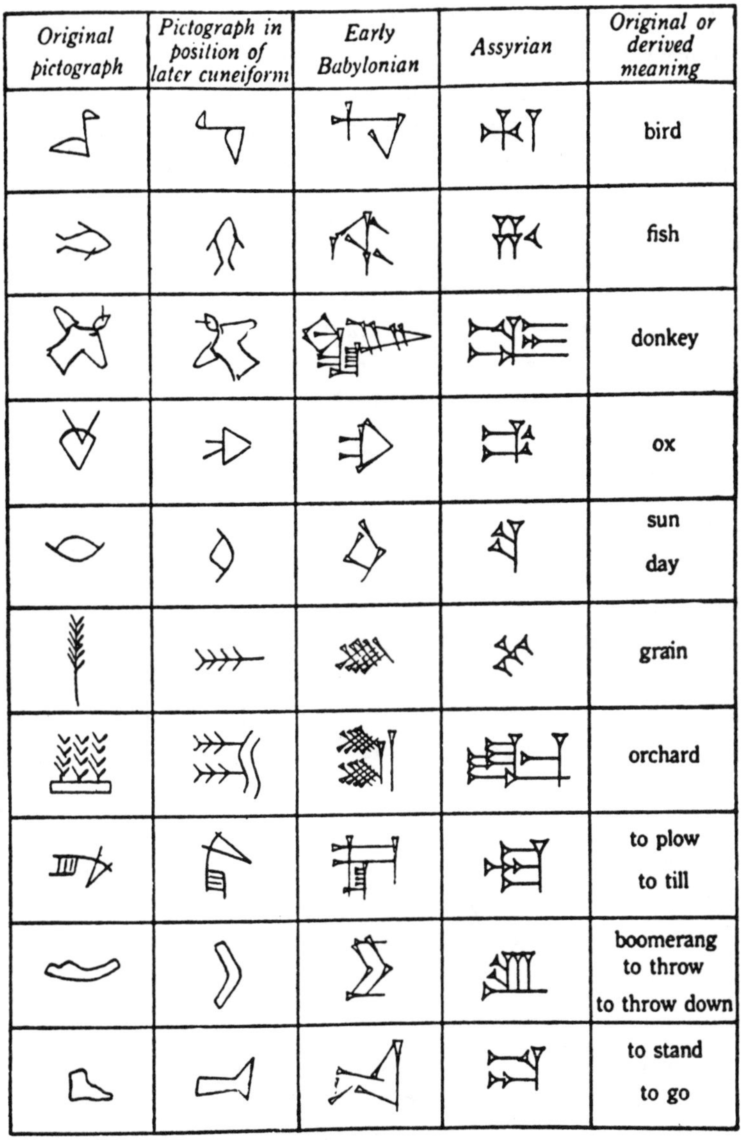

Original pictograph	Pictograph in position of later cuneiform	Early Babylonian	Assyrian	Original or derived meaning
				bird
				fish
				donkey
				ox
				sun day
				grain
				orchard
				to plow to till
				boomerang to throw to throw down
				to stand to go

Figure 1   Sumer: First Writing

The origin and development of a few cuneiform characters, from the early Sumerian to their classical Assyrian representation.

(from *They Wrote on Clay* by Edward Chiera. Courtesy University of Chicago Press.)

cate, these tablets of pictographs at least suggested to the memory what would have been almost impossible to remember precisely. Again, in business transactions, two individuals might remember purely verbal agreements differently. "Put it in writing" was probably an early requirement.

The pictographs, however, were inefficient. As with the hieroglyphics of the Egyptians, a picture that represented a spoken word was often ambiguous. A picture of the sun could represent our hot star or a male child, two very different meanings. Gradually, for the sake of speed, the scribes stylized the pictures into symbols. So too, words that sounded alike and would apparently utilize the same picture could be slightly altered to account for the different meanings, e.g., "sun" or "son."

Edward Chiera, the great scholar of Sumerian, tells how a scribe might resolve a knotty problem in inscribing a clay tablet representing an important business transaction: The seller of the product is named Kuraka. Not having an alphabetic rendering of this name to imprint into the clay, the ingenious scribe must make do with the available pictographs. He inscribes the symbol for "mountain" (*kur*), then "water" (*a*), finally "mouth" (*ka*). Before these three symbols he inscribes a small sign which to other scribes means "watch it, don't take what follows literally." He means that he is not writing "mountain-water-mouth" as initiating the business transaction but rather a man whose name sounds like these three signs put together.

How long do you think it took before other scribes, exasperated by these and other prickly little problems, began to translate the pictures directly into their phonetic equivalents? Instead of visual signs of *things*, they would make visual signs of *sounds*, i.e., of spoken language. In this case, it was strings of signs for the different consonant syllables with their visually unexpressed vowel modifications, e.g., "ca(se)," "co(unt)," "cou(gh)," "ce(nt)," "cou(ld)."

Figure 2   Greek Linear B
A Linear B tablet unearthed at Pylos on the Greek mainland. It illustrates an inventory of tripods and vases with their written descriptions.

(from *The Mycenaeans* by Lord William Taylour. Courtesy Thames and Hudson.)

There is an interesting lesson in the evolution of writing in terms of its social function. Whether in the Near East or on Crete (where "Linear B" tablets from c. 1400 B.C. were found and subsequently identified as an early Greek dialect, as translated by Michael Ventris in the 1950's), the purpose of writing seems first to have been commercial—warehouse inventories, trade accounts, tax records, and the like. Only later did civilized people realize that there were even more powerful civilizational uses for written language—poetry, myth, history, theogony.

This example from the evolution of human civilization should warn us about our obsessive practicality. Indeed the education of the young Sumerian aristocrats early in the development of writing evolved into the development and study of their traditions and chronicles. Education in schools soon displaced the utilitarian with literary, historical, and other value-oriented studies. These were the materials that this supremely talented ethnic group thought to be important for a useful life.

The need to order and simplify also underlies the evolution of written speech. In the next phase of writing, increasing attempts were made to link spoken sound to written symbol. Thus we see among the Semitic languages of west Asia increasing use of syllabaries which while not completely efficient were a real advance over the pictographic stage even when abstract signs substituted for real objects. The Babylonian consonant syllabaries still did not show the vowel sounds as written symbols. They were implied in the various signs for consonant syllables. But, as we now realize, the logic inherent in the written sign-to-sound relationship would lead to a more efficient writing system consisting of all the consonant and vowel sounds. Until the end, the Semites refused to go along with the advance. As in Hebrew, the vowels would have to be inferred. Only consonants would be printed.

The Greeks were responsible for this crucial breakthrough. Such Semitic letters that they adapted from the Phoenicians as "aleph," "beth," "gimel," became "alpha," "beta," "gamma." This important simplification opened the worlds of writing and reading to a much wider public. Later it made possible the kinds of large-scaled schooling that the Romans put into effect in their Empire. In effect, the alphabet paved the way for the mass semiliteracy of our own day.

Writing and reading advanced beyond their basic commercial applications almost immediately as they were discovered in each society. Their practitioners organized themselves into secret guild-like professions. The scribes, as in the Near East and Egypt, were often at once members of their respective religious communities. Thus, quickly following came the codification of the religious and historical tradition of each society, along with its poetry, myth, and literature. What we witness in this evolution from the practical to the holy and the beautiful is the gradual realization of the versatility of written language to reveal the complexity of thought and the varied interests of human beings.

The Sumerian schools early created institutions that prepared one of the most important and high-born citizens of their society, the scribe, who was at once sage, professor, holy man, ambassador, and artist. In China, which later evolved its own unique patterns of writing after 1500 B.C., the written word was almost continuously in the possession of the Mandarin classes, which exercised vast powers to control the destiny of their society. Worshipping the wise and educated, the Chinese placed enormous esthetic and moral value on these purveyors of established law, ritual, and tradition. The Chinese logography—the particular writing system (graphemes)—was likewise a difficult, inaccessible code whose use was reserved for only the most able and fortunate survivors of the state examination system.

The Chinese logographs were essentially words or meanings. Unlike the Semitic consonant syllabaries or the Greek and Latin alphabet, the logographs had no built-in phonetic equivalents. The Chinese had made the jump from a pictographic language—pictures of things—to perhaps the most abstract written system we know. Some scholars (Sapir, Cassirer) have looked to Chinese as the most purely semantic of all meaning-oriented written systems in that it has practically no grammar built into it.

First, as noted above, the logographs have no phonetic equivalents. Second, since each sign is a word or meaning (with modifiers), each sentence is a series of concepts that calls upon the reader to supply the syntactic relationships (the modifying articles, prepositions, pronouns). Unlike written English which is built up out of twenty-six letters, Chinese requires a memory knowledge of literally thousands of logographs. No wonder that the literary scholars, the survivors of the medieval examination system, were so highly respected as sages.

Mandarin Chinese thus could be maintained over the centuries; it was a strong leash on progress. Citizens of Canton and Shanghai, whose respective colloquial spoken expression had evolved along separate paths, found that their dialects were mutually incomprehensible. Both could apply local phonetic elements, however, to the neutral Mandarin written form and thus understand the written language, while not understanding each others' spoken equivalents of the written texts. Certainly classical Chinese has never been a written language intended for mass literacy and education.

Literacy's Date with History

At one time, highly intelligent, highly skilled artisans, warriors, even political leaders did not need to be literate. Today, to be able to read and write fluently is a precondition for success and fulfillment in our increasingly complex, technological world. It has been long coming, but now the requirements of literacy overwhelm us.

Where once reading teachers worried about the stifling of reading progress due to the emotional or family problems of the young, today the equation is put another way. We now know better. There is no easily identifiable cause-and-effect relationship between emotional difficulties and reading success. Some suffer harrowing home difficulties, yet learn to read with ease. Other children, coming from wonderfully supportive families, in harmony with themselves and others, undergo terrible difficulties, suffering handicaps that require immediate intervention.

Yet one part of the equation still holds true, and with a special twist. We can predict the effect on any child, whether placid, active, neurotic, or phlegmatic, who in the first or second grade has difficulty learning to read. Lack of reading success in an environment in which reading is a criterion of educational advance is sure to result in sometimes unsolvable emotional overtones. No child leaves the classroom unscathed who suffers through the reading lesson.

No longer can one withdraw into a niche as an auto mechanic, waiter, construction foreman. Today's world is constructed out of letters. From these flow ancillary symbolic constructions, mathematical formuli, musical notations, computer and logical patterns. An individual's intelligence may be inherently powerful, but it remains a dulled tool without the precision of thought given to it by written language.

It is a long journey since the days of the Greeks, when the educated had a curriculum demanding immensely different skills and human values. They tell the story of the Athenian admiral Themistocles, who in 480 B.C. engineered one of the most supreme strategic and tactical victories the world has seen—the defeat of the allied Persian Armada at Salamis off the coast of Athens.

The Athenians, who had abandoned their city before the advancing Persian host, returned to Athens in glory, the highly appreciated and heroic Themistocles in the vanguard. A great festivity held by the aristocrats of the city was one of the first events to follow the restoration of the city. Themistocles was to be a guest of honor. As was usual among the educated classes, at the close of the meal, wine was poured and lyres were taken up and passed from individual to individual to play and sing, perhaps an immortal stanza from one of the poets—Homer, Hesiod, Pindar.

When the lyre was at last passed to Themistocles, he shrank back and in profound embarrassment waved the musical instrument away. Growing up in a democratizing city such as Athens, he had been able to advance to splendid heights of command on the power of his intelligence, leadership, bravery. However, in his youth, poverty had forced his family to forego the proper education for a young man of aristocratic pretensions. Such an education would have included musical and literary instruction. Now, faced with aristocratic achievements in his own right, Themistocles could only confront his peers with plebian incoherency.

Could Themistocles have advanced to chief petty officer in today's navy without formal educational credentials? Probably not. But it does no good to complain that implacable certification limitations and requirements have replaced what was once a natural give-and-take of intelligence and talent. We now require union cards, diplomas, and degrees. Reading is an essential prerequisite. Masses of people, diminishing resources, the new knowledge industries and the skilled purveyors of their techniques, signal the shape of leadership and survival in the future.

Conclusion

If you are reading this book, you are probably aware that the teaching of reading is a subject that has experienced much controversy. Also you may expect that a book on reading would of necessity be normative or directive, have something to propose. For, while we have been experiencing a narrowing of the vocational skills market to the traditional academic pathways created by the literate classes, we are, at the same time, glimpsing the beginning of a new breakthrough in reading.

This advance in understanding may never result in great remedial success for many an incipient scholar. However it bodes to yield a deeper and wider understanding of the human capacity to read. More important, it could create an ecumenical consensus as to the nature of the reading process. Thus we may here be at a happy moment in reading education, one which may end a one-hundred-and-fifty-year heritage of conflict and educational chaos.

FURTHER READINGS

Chadwick, John. (1967) *The decipherment of Linear B.* Cambridge: Cambridge University Press.

Chiera, Edward. (1938) *They wrote on clay.* Chicago: University of Chicago Press.

Marshack, Alexander. (1972) *The roots of civilization.* New York: McGraw Hill.

Resnick, D. P. and L. B. Resnick. (1977) "The nature of literacy: An historical explanation," *Harvard Educational Review.* Vol. 47, 370-385.

3

The Reading Wars

A Lesson from the Deaf

CONFLICT IS OFTEN the price of progress. However, the jolt that stirred the dust in reading instruction was a gentle and intellectual one. Let us look back to the 1820's, Hartford, Connecticut. Yes, New England, the ferment of the early industrial revolution, the source of so much energy and change. The Reverend Thomas Gallaudet was nearing the completion of a long and dedicated teaching career in the Asylum for the Deaf and Dumb. This institution was not to be a mere trash receptacle for the tragic unwanted. Here the wounded and afflicted would, under his guidance, receive an education that God and duty had foreordained for all His children. Gallaudet's institution was to be a school as well as an asylum.

With energy and ingenuity, he had labored long and hard to find a means to teach these youngsters to read so that they too might have the word of God at first hand. To break through the implacable barrier of sensory deprivation, of deafness that struck away their language, almost their humanity, was his dream. With power of will and intellect, Gallaudet came up with a technique that seemed to work; at least it partially circumvented the awful blockage that deafness and speechlessness present for the acquistion of literacy.

By the early 1830's, Gallaudet was retired, his work hardly noticed, his squireship of the Asylum now in younger hands. Might not his educational work with the afflicted be of use to those now laboring with such energy in the creation of a common school? Thus came into being a modest work, *A Mother's Primer*, in which the whole-word method of instruction was set forth much as Gallaudet had presented it to his deaf wards. Only now it was to be used by mothers, teachers, educators all, and for all children.

The book reached Boston, then in the throes of building a school system for an expanding community, with many children of poor and working-class parents. A group of educators was dispatched to Hartford both to consult with Reverend Gallaudet and to see how his method was still being applied by the teachers at the Asylum. The report was favorable. With the approval of the newly-appointed Secretary of the Massachusetts Board of Education, Horace Mann, the Boston School Committee gave its consent for several experimental classrooms to be converted to Gallaudet's whole-word method of reading.

In these classes, the children, instead of learning the names of the letters and their sounds, then gradually combining the letters and sounds into words, finally memorizing the rules by which the different sounds were elicited from the same letters and from different letters, would learn to recognize words by sight alone. By this method, the visual shape of words would create an engram of memory and the whole word would be spoken and understood. No more tedious memorization of letters and their sounds. However, it was just an experiment, in a dynamic and experimenting community. This was in 1837.

A few years later, in 1843, Horace Mann had the Commonwealth of Massachusetts in turmoil with his surging enthusiasms: a specified and established school year, in-service training for teachers, sequential and required curricula, school libraries, and, everywhere, advocacy for community self-taxation for the support of these common schools.

In this same year, Mann went abroad to observe personally the best in education in Scotland, Prussia, and other nations on the Continent. On his return, he issued his seventh annual report (January 1844). In terms of organization, discipline, teacher training, Mann felt that Europeans were far ahead of even the jewel of the Massachusetts system, Boston. While the critique of the Boston School System was incidental to his praise of the European systems, it allowed the conservative schoolmasters to admonish Mann for his ardent enthusiasms, especially the whole-word method, which he continued to push: "how can a child to whom nature offers such a profusion of beautiful objects—of sights and sounds and colors,—and in whose breast so many social feelings spring up;—how can such a child be expected to [learn] with delight from all these stiff and lifeless columns of the alphabet?" (Mann)

The Boston Association of Masters assigned Samuel Greene, principal of the Phillips Grammar School, to write a critique. It was long and detailed, showing the failings of the whole-word method both as an organizational system for teaching reading and for the consequent "great neglect of spelling." In the end, Greene claimed that the whole-word method resulted in little scholastic progress and "the task of teaching the alphabet, and the art of combining letters into words, [was made] more difficult, and less satisfactory, than if the child had begun with the letters."

Further, Greene later argued, why adopt a method originally developed for use with the deaf and dumb in the education of the normal? "On the same principle, and with about as good reason, might one urge the general adoption of a book prepared with raised letters for the blind, because the sense of touch quickened as if to supply that of sight. . . ."

It was not merely a new and possibly tainted reading method, partially foisted upon them by a zealous and preachy educational reformer (Horace Mann) that bothered them. Here, in a time when the status of educators was rising because of great social need, the comfortable school system itself was being rocked by an impudent educational theorizer, namely Mr. Horace Mann.

No clear victor emerged from the battle. Horace Mann eventually left to become president of the first coeducational college west of the Appalachians, Antioch College. Samuel Greene became a professor of didactics at Brown University. Soon common schools, curricula, textbooks were being put into use all over the country. Practically every community by necessity had its own innovators in dealing with wholly unique educational needs.

Time and history have their impact on the immediacy of old debates. America and American education were in ferment in those decades before and after the Civil War. The necessities of literacy were even then becoming clearly urgent in the modernizing society. Hundreds of thousands, even millions of immigrants, farm laborers, urban factory workers yearned to be taught to read. And so instruction in the three R's got on, in one way or another, mostly by dint of traditional practice. Eventually the issue of methods of teaching reading would have to be taken up again.

The Scientific Spirit

Let us go forward again, about forty years, to the mid-1880's. The United States was undergoing the high tide of industrial and national expansion. Science, knowledge, and technological innovations surged through the American consciousness. Millions of immigrants washed onto our shores each year. The American state-supported public school system had now begun to supplant the reforming ideal of the early Common School.

From St. Louis kindergartens to Baltimore graduate schools (Johns Hopkins), the educational mania shrieked progress. In 1874, the Michigan Supreme Court gave the final okay for what was already the dominant secondary school, the public tax-supported high school. By 1890, over 200,000 pupils would be attending this new growth institution. Graduate schools of education in New York, Missouri, and Michigan were rapidly taking shape, expanding beyond the traditional normal school training of teachers.

It is evident that a readiness to search out and apply this new scientific knowledge to education had become a passionate commitment. In this setting we can understand the work of James McKeen Cattell. Born in 1860, son of the president of Lafayette College, Cattell completed his undergraduate and master's work at Lafayette, continuing his graduate study alternately at the new Johns Hopkins University in Baltimore and with Wilhelm Wundt in Leipzig. Cattell was of the same precocious generation as the educational philosopher John Dewey (born 1859). Cattell published two papers, in 1885 and 1886, (when he was age 25), the results of his laboratory research work with Wundt in Leipzig. The first, on reaction time, as influenced by the intensity of stimuli, was one of the earliest pieces of experimental work in the area that has again come alive in the measurement of intelligence in the 1980's. The second, on letter and word perception, caused a stir as its implications were gradually disseminated following its publication in *Mind*.

The key quotation from "The Time It Takes to See and Name Objects" follows:

> I find it takes about twice as long to read (aloud, as fast as possible) words which have no connexion as words which

make sentences, and letters which have no connexion as letters which make words. When the words make sentences and the letters words, not only do the process of seeing and naming overlap, but by one mental effort the subject can recognize a whole group of words or letters, and by one will-act choose the motion to be made in naming them, so that the rate at which the words and letters are read is really only limited by the maximum rapidity at which the speech-organs can be moved. (Dennis, 1948, pp. 327-328)

The revolving drum device, on which Cattell had pasted letters, observed as they passed by a slit in a screen at various rates of speed, later was perfected and called the "tachistoscope." What this and other confirming experiments seem to argue is that the whole word, not the letter, is the more perfect unit of reading comprehension. Further, words in intelligible order—sentences—could be read more easily and accurately in a given time sequence than random words.

Educators quickly saw the implications, that letter and phonic identification, even if they did appear to support spelling skills, were inefficient. Letter and phonic identification seemed to slow down reading comprehension, much as Horace Mann had intuitively argued, even on the basis of evidence from deaf children.

This was an era of transition, moving from the localized publishing of school texts—for example, the McGuffey Readers—to the beginning of national textbook companies. It was not long before the so-called basal readers appeared, which consisted of a series of sequential readers from primers to more advanced upper-grade literature. These changes were not the result merely of a crucial experiment by James M. Cattell, nor of the enthusiasms of another reforming New England educator, Francis Parker (born 1837, New Hampshire), who proclaimed the new educational ideas from Chicago's first teachers college. There were many other enthusiastic educators.

G. Stanley Hall, born in Ashfield, Massachusetts, in

1844, had set up one of the first psychological laboratories in the United States at Johns Hopkins University. Here, Dewey, Cattell, and later Edmund B. Huey (*The Psychology and Pedagogy of Reading*, 1907) absorbed the experimentalist, scientific attitudes that would argue for the whole-word reading method (look-say) and a controlled sight vocabulary. The weight of opinion of these scientist/educators training a generation of aspiring public school teachers would eventually sway the education of millions of American children.

"Look-Say" Reigns on High

A two-thousand-year-old tradition of reading pedagogy dies hard. The teaching of letter names, their sounds, and the dozens of rules by which words could be analyzed into their phonic components, and then tediously compared mentally with the spoken equivalents was probably the educational norm in American schools between 1885 and 1925. By the mid-twenties, however, a profession of education was becoming conscious of itself. It was establishing itself along the lines of scholarship, searching for new psychological knowledge to apply to the teaching/learning situation; it sought to become an educational discipline having independence of judgment and action. Perhaps above all, the teaching profession now saw itself as a force for social and political modernization in the United States.

Reading textbook writers during this period were trumpeting the equivalent of Dick, Jane and Spot for the sight-reading of beginners, the colleges of education pouring out zealous professionals who looked disdainfully on the old phonics approach. At the same time, the "Progressive Education Association" was making an uneasy alliance with a variety of politically liberal unions and civic groups. "Dare the

School Change the Social Order" was the provocative title of
one important pamphlet (1931) by educational philosopher
George Counts of Teachers College, Columbia University.
No one can say for sure why there began an unfortunate association of a reading method—the whole-word/look-say
method—with a profession that only at the top leadership
levels could be said to have a political coloration.

An interesting sample of the ultimate drift of the whole-
word/look-say method of teaching reading during this period
is a passage written by the distinguished educationist, Arthur
I. Gates, in his book, *New Methods in Primary Reading.*
Writing in 1928, Gates already saw some of the explanatory
weakness in whole-word identification and the simultaneous
comprehension that supposedly accompanies this perceived
identification of the word.

> "Although thought getting and word mastery are still consid-
> ered separate tasks, the emphasis has recently been changing.
> An increasing number of teachers are now emphasizing com-
> prehension from the beginning. . . . In the extreme case, train-
> ing in word mastery is dispensed with entirely. This practice
> is defended by the assumption that when proper provision for
> the exercise of comprehension is made the pupil will "natural-
> ly" or "incidentally" acquire a sufficient degree of skill in
> word perception." (p. 2)

It wasn't until the 1950's that the reading wars heated up
to the levels of the early-nineteenth-century Massachusetts
debates. The American educational system had matured in
the 1940's, the school population having leveled off during
this decade. The fifties were a period of cold war political re-
activity. Then came Sputnik, which exacerbated the debate.
Research had clearly shown that the educational levels of the
fifties, as compared with the prewar generation, had not really advanced. Moreover, in the 1950's, for the first time, our
technological and political hegemony in the world was being
challenged, then by the Soviets.

The education profession, especially its training of teachers in life adjustment, progressive education, was bitterly attacked by liberal arts traditionalists. Books such as *Educational Wastelands* (1953) by Arthur Bestor attacked the thin content of lower school curricula, the intellectual shallowness that characterized the education of teachers. Organizations such as the *Council for Basic Education* focused both on the politicized nature of the profession and on the philosophical leadership of secular liberals such as the venerable John Dewey and William H. Kilpatrick.

The back-to-basics movement of political and educational conservatives had only here and there taken potshots at the whole-word recognition method and the consequent neglect of phonics. The phonics program had retained its nostalgia for many parents who had been exposed to it in the good old days. Rudolf Flesch's book, *Why Johnny Can't Read* (1955), brought it all to the surface and with heat. The reason *why* was obvious—a lack of systematic phonics instruction in the reading program. As Samuel Blumenfeld would later document, the decline of reading in the generation between 1930 and the mid-fifties, a period when the education profession's curricular command over the public schools was complete, could be laid at the door of the professional educator's politically "biased" approaches to reading instruction.

Take, for example, the Scott-Foresman readers edited by William Gray. Gray, at the University of Chicago, was a dean of the School of Education, once under John Dewey's institutional leadership. In its 1930 primers this series introduced sixty-nine new words in thirty-nine pages with a total of 565 repetitions using these sixty-nine new words.

By the 1950's when the method would have been thought to be developed so that it was more efficient, the new-word count had dropped to fifty-eight. The number of repetitions had increased to 2613 total words to which the youngsters were exposed, and, of course, the total number of pages thus covered (172) had risen, necessitating several additional books to cover the basic reading materials. (Blumenfeld, 1973, pp. 162-163) In fact, if one examines a primer of the early sixties, it is evident that the critiques had largely gone over the heads of the series publishers, as the new-word count continued to drop in absolute numbers as well as pro-portionally to the repetitions. The total sight vocabulary ex-pected of youngsters in the early grades thus was meager.

The dissolution of the hold of look-say instruction was ad-mittedly slow. The publishers Merrill and Lippincott, among others, had introduced more phonically-oriented series, but the training of teachers who might someday rewrite the older series was obviously still in the hands of the old guard. Change unfortunately seemed slow in coming. Yet, the con-flict in the media was hot and heavy. In fact it would not be and exaggeration to say that the war over educational achievement, teacher training, curricular reform, educational institutional support and expansion was so intense that it threatened to paralyze the whole public educational enter-prise. Attacks by Hyman Rickover, the father of the nuclear submarine, were especially potent and did much to center public attention on the issue of educational standards in cross-national comparisons.

The Carnegie Corporation commissioned James Conant, former president of Harvard, High Commissioner in Occu-pied West Germany after World War II, to undertake an ecumenical examination of American education. His books, *Slums and Suburbs* (1961) and *The American High School* (1959), did much to bring peace to the scene and to focus on general educational reform, especially in foreign language, biological science, and mathematics programs.

Unfortunately for all of these serious moves to study the problem of curricular and methodological reform, the coun-terculture movement of the late sixties now moved in to add a radically different social ingredient to the educational fer-ment of the day. In a sense, it left a greater educational legacy for the last two decades of twentieth-century education than that of either the older progressivists or their conservative antagonists.

For one, the actual debate over reading methodology was smothered in anti-school rhetoric. In the vain attempt to stem a tidal wave of disintegrating academic standards, the reform of reading pedagogy could not be central. How could reading be important, so the countercultural messiahs intoned, when the child was "being oppressed by the school"?

The Final Twist

However, other things were happening on the reading scene that would have their impact. The first was another Carnegie Foundation study on education. This one, on reading, was directed by Jeanne Chall, first of the City College of New York, subsequently at the Harvard Graduate School of Education. The second was more a movement within the scholarly disciplines. This was the realization that the problem of reading was part of the larger aspect of the study of human language. The joining of many linguistic scholars for the debate over reading was to bring a fascinating and ultimately decisive dimension to the reading wars.

Jeanne Chall's study was concluded in 1967 with the publication of her book, *Learning to Read: The Great Debate.* In this book, Chall surveyed the various research studies concerning the effectiveness of the differing reading approaches. Her recommendation, after she had weighed the evidence of innumerable studies as well as the new writing of linguists who were now entering the fray, was, simply, an emphasis in beginning reading on the decoding process. Further, she argued that the more efficient and successful patterns of teaching reading in the ten or fifteen years since the debate had been reopened pointed to the old phonics approach.

What decoding meant was that the child in looking at the letters and words would be taught to translate the visual signs into phonic or audible equivalents. In learning the necessary rules to do this in an irregularly structured language such as English, the child would have to be taught the phonic rules—blends, diagraphs, vowel combinations. Having decoded to sound, the child would then be able to relate this sound to the equivalent vocal representative of his natural spoken language (just as the ancient Sumerians had had to do). Comprehension of the written material would then take place.

Predictably, the advocates of the whole-word/sight approach to reading replied with a volley of statistics that were persuasive enough to counter Chall's evidence. (Albert Harris for one turned out to be a potent opponent.) (Harris, 1970, pp. 75-79) One can say that the result of the Carnegie Foundation attempt at ecumenism in reading had succeeded only to the extent that it validated whatever each school community, in its political thrashings could arrive at as a majority force in shaping curricular development. It at least gave some dignity to the polemicist phonics people. It did not, in retrospect, completely pull the rug out from under the whole-word/look-say advocates. The textbook publishers were still in turmoil.

More important was the entrance of a number of linguistic scholars into the reading debate. Authorities such as Leonard Bloomfield and Charles Fries were joined by a variety of educators not merely to produce treatises on such topics as "Language and Reading" or "Linguistics and Reading," but, even more interestingly, to try their hands at developing text materials for the classroom, "Basic Reading," Lippincott, (Fries), 1963, 1969; "Linguistic Readers," Merrill, (Bloomfield), 1966. As we will develop later on, these writings did lend a wholly new atmosphere to the discussions as they moved away from conservative and liberal political jeremiads to the scholars' world of research, study, and experimentation.

The so-called phonics/linguistics approach favored by Bloomfield and Fries was an intellectualized version of the old phonics method, now with theoretical as well as practical validation. While publishers such as Merrill and Lippincott rapidly jumped on the wagon, other giants held back. Most older teachers were set with the traditional look-say basal reading text, and teacher training departments were unlikely to move rapidly in a new direction, especially such a seemingly conservative one. Publishers did, however, steadily add to their phonics components in elementary reading texts. The result of this eclecticism was that it began to blur the clarity of method that had at least provided consistency in the look-say tradition.

In 1971 Frank Smith published his college text, *Understanding Reading*. This book summarized in a tantalizingly suggestive manner the developments in another wing of linguistic thought. The research in this area would impact on our understanding of the process of teaching reading. The so-called psycholinguistic school, whose breakthrough scholar Noam Chomsky had put the older behavioristic psychological version of language acquisition and structure to flight, e.g., B. F. Skinner, had in one short burst of research completed an end run around the other positions.

Indeed, almost over night, Bloomfield and Fries were passé. A behavioristic perceptual researcher had also recently moved into this cognitive position held by psycholinguistics: Eleanor Gibson argued that, on the basis of her perceptual research, the processing of knowledge seemed to take place autonomously within the person rather than as a response to external stimulation. In her *Psychology of Reading* (1975), with Harry Levin, she further added to the psycholinguistic sweep.

Teachers and scholars in reading were quick to realize how much light the new psycholinguistics could throw on so many controversial questions about the nature of the reading process. It was primarily Frank Smith who, in *Understanding Reading* as well as an accompanying edited volume, *Psycholinguistics and Reading,* showed that there was here a highly developed theory of language, child language acquisition, and the perceptual process of transferring the visual signs of language into meaning that potentially could be translated into a pedagogy of reading.

Among the publishers, Scott-Foresman, long the flagship of reading series and the whole-word approach, moved into the breach. Included in the sponsors and designers of this series was a number of psycholinguists and reading luminaries—Kenneth Goodman, Helen Robinson, Joseph Wepman. The series, "Reading Unlimited," 1976, however, contained within it more verbalizations of psycholinguistic theory than their realization in curricular and pedagogical approach. Simply, the meaning of this new theory for reading was not yet clear. There were still more important problems to be solved with regard to the application in the classroom beyond what had been developed by Frank Smith, Kenneth Goodman, and others.

It can be said, however, that within the profession, the psycholinguistic model swept the day. The *Reading Research Quarterly* in the 1970's was filled with research studies that confirmed the predictions of psycholinguists. Certainly the whole-word advocates within the profession were converted, if indeed many of them had to be retrained to understand the subtleties of the new theory. College textbooks in reading still often gave lip service to "linguistics," with little inner understanding of what was happening.

The phonics, decoding conservatives, saw psycholinguistics as a great challenger. Frank Smith had derrogated systematic phonics instruction unmercifully. Thus we still do find in the late seventies and early eighties, holdouts for the decoding approach, including Jeanne Chall herself. Still, if we may paraphrase a teacher returning from a reading conference: "Psycholinguistics is where reading is."

FURTHER READINGS

Bloomfield, L. and C. Barnhart. (1961) *Let's read: A linguistic approach.* Detroit: Wayne State University Press.

Blumenfeld, Samuel L. (1973) *The new illiterates.* New Rochelle: Arlington House.

Chall, Jeanne. (1967) *Learning to read: The great debate.* New York: McGraw Hill.

Dennis, Wayne. ed., (1948) *Readings in the history of psychology.* New York: Appleton, Century, Crofts.

Flesch, Rudolf. (1955) *Why Johnny can't read and what you can do about it.* New York: Harper.

Fries, Charles C. (1962) *Linguistics and reading.* New York: Holt, Rinehart, and Winston.

Gates, Arthur I. (1928) *New methods in primary reading.* New York: Columbia University Press.

Gibson, Eleanor J. and Harry Levin. (1975) *The psychology of reading.* Cambridge, Mass.: MIT Press.

Harris, Albert J. (1970) *How to increase reading ability.* (5th ed.) New York: David McKay.

Huey, E. B. (1968) *The psychology and pedagogy of reading.* Cambridge, Mass.: MIT Press. [1907]

Krug, Edward A. (1969) *The shaping of the American high school.* Madison: University of Wisconsin Press.

Mathews, Mitford M. (1966) *Teaching to read: Historically considered.* Chicago: University of Chicago Press.

4

Language, the Clue

Call of the Wild?

THE IMPORTANCE OF psycholinguistics to reading instruction is that here, for the first time, we have a general theory of human thinking and learning that has had much scientific empirical and practical confirmation. In the past we had to rely on a tradition of reading instruction that was derived from the Romans. It seemed eventually to work for most children, but tediously, and it often required much unnecessary disciplinary severity. Letters and sounds are certainly part of the process of learning to read, but for many children, the price was too high.

Innovative spirits such as Thomas Gallaudet or Horace Mann could not be blamed if they sought new ideas and practices from such an awkward-seeming source—the instruction of the deaf. What the insights from experience in teaching deaf children gave these gentlemen was a new yardstick for measuring reading progress. Agreed, deaf children could not hear sounds and were dependent on their visual skills to learn the different shapes of words and their meanings. However normal children had eyes as well and could also be taught to distinguish the shapes of words. Again, instruction in letter names and sounds was so often painful.

Others would argue differently. The limited and specialized experiences of deaf children could not constitute an explanation or rationale for the instruction of hearing children. After all, it is a fact that not even all hearing children take to the whole-word/sight approach.

James Cattell's tachistoscope gave us more perspective on the value of teaching children to read words and sentences rather than starting with letters. Intriguing as Cattell's scientific experiments were, they didn't tell us why we read words and sentences more easily than letters. Though modern educators for over two generations opted for the whole-word/sight approach, the general lowering of reading levels discerned in the 1950's, when our public educational system had come to maturity, should have been a warning.

The tragedy in all this internecine warfare was that somewhere along the way the battle between two particular and special approaches to reading instruction took on the coloration of the larger and irrelevant political/education wars, between liberals as sight-word advocates and conservatives as adorers of the phonics approach. Even today, now that psycholinguistics has won a scholarly consensus, outside the teaching profession are some who would once more interject irrelevant political factionalism into this crucial social area (literacy).

Psycholinguistics has absorbed the work of child development theorists, neurologists, perceptual psychologists, language pathologists—such as on aphasia and dyslexia—and, especially, that from linguistics itself. Reading, as we know, is a form of language use. To understand how the child both learns to read and then progresses to higher levels of literacy, we need to study not only the process of reading but, more generally, how the child becomes a language learner. Then we can approach the mysteries of reading, mysteries that have evaded the preliterate majority of human beings who have lived on this earth since writing and reading were first invented.

Some have argued that the theoretical turning point in the language debates came in 1959 when Noam Chomsky wrote a thirty-two-page critique for the journal *Language* of a new book by the then-preeminent psychologist B. F. Skinner. This book, *Verbal Behavior,* was touted as the capstone in Skinner's long career in developing his version of behavioristic psychology. The model of "operant conditioning" which he applied to such a human phenomenon as language was supposed to naturalize once and for all this human/cultural entity.

This endeavor had been tried before, by John Watson, and mainly Leonard Bloomfield. Skinner's enterprise, however, was the most ambitious. Not impartial students of the subject have likened Chomsky's review to a shark taking huge bites from a helpless whale. Two decades later, it is still clear that the Skinnerian view of mind and language no longer "bakes bread." It is not useful as a way of making good predictions about the reading process.

What the behaviorists, including Skinner, had long attempted was to bring the seemingly unique mental behavior of man into the natural biological world by joining the principles of animal instinct to human motivations. The model was primarily the animal response system. Operant conditioning demonstrated how living things could be channeled in their behavior, e.g., "chaining," in which the proper stimuli would elicit programmable behavior, by releasing a creature's basic survivalistic instinct.

The Skinnerian view of language likewise had an outside/inside perspective, i.e., the language that we used was what was supposedly elicited by others through the proper externally applied stimuli. The child supposedly learns to speak in a social environment in order to respond to certain life sustaining situations. Mysterious things like thought, subjectivity, and creativity would be shown to be really overt responses to particular externally applied challenges—stimuli—so as to reduce or satisfy the basic needs of the human animal. Human language could in the Skinnerian model be shown to be a mere elaboration of more general forms of animal communication. Human language then reduces to a form of behavior whose overriding function is to serve the clear-cut survival needs of the individual—food, shelter, procreation. Language in this view was for humans what howls, screams, calls, were for animals.

The persuasiveness of the behavioristic approach to language—after all, we are animals, even with language, aren't we?—was shared by many scholars in the field. The various linguistic reading series that appeared in the sixties and early seventies in response to the search for a more ecumenical approach to reading were essentially built out of this behavioristic model of thought and language.

In the Bloomfield-Fries-Merrill readers, the child was exposed to strings of phonic family elements: "cat," "pat," "rat"; "see," "me," "he," "gee"; "cold," "cup," "can." The theory was that since the written form of language was built out of sound or phonic elements derived from the natural spoken language, drilling the child in phonic families would assist future recognition of sight/sound/meaning patterns.

In fact, Charles Walcutt, who was a principal author of the Lippincott reading series, specifically said in his reading text, *Reading, a Phonic-Linguistic Approach* (1974), that writing was the visual form of spoken language. When we read, we essentially decode visual signs to sounds, listen to what we have decoded (subvocally), and subsequently comprehend the material. This, of course, was the basic position in support of phonics instruction to which Jeanne Chall had given her imprimatur in her Carnegie Foundation research project, *Learning to Read: the Great Debate* (1967).

The point of the phonics/linguistic pedagogy approach was to drill the child, imprinting these phonic rules and regularities. Once conditioned to respond to these sound/visual signs (letters), the child would then associate sight ("cat," "pat," "fat") to sound, then think about the natural spoken language that he/she experiences in the real world of conversation, speaking, and listening. The result would be to understand the world through "reading" its associated sounds. The reader should note that these theoretical approaches to human behavior and language were not merely the abstractions and obsessions of scholars. They began to have real pedagogical and curricular consequences in the classroom. As much rode on the truth and thus the success of these presuppositions as rode on the supposed educational significance of Cattell's tachistoscope experiments in the mid-1880's.

We need not go into the details of Chomsky's dismemberment of Skinner's theory of language. The thrust of Chomsky's analysis was to show that the process described in the conditioned, chaining behavior of animals, could not be applied to the facts of human language. Chomsky argued that Skinner's basic model, even within its own world of assumptions and rules, was shot through with fallacious reasoning. When applied to humans, it warped and indeed falsified the facts of verbal behavior as we all know and experience them.

By contrast, the picture of the human mind that was emerging in the new psycholinguistics had much in common with traditional cognitive psychology. It attempted to stay within the realities of human mentation, to view thought as something uniquely different from orthodox animal instinctive behavior.

Chomsky, however, was already going beyond traditional cognitive psychological research to a larger perspective in which he argued for the unique internal character of thought and language. We are not the products of our conditioning. Language and thought unfold in an individual autonomous manner, perhaps *sui generis*, only to man. These mysteries could not be revealed by comparing humans with the behavioral template of pigeons, rats, or even chimpanzees. Perhaps reading itself was a dramatic and special aspect of man's own place in nature.

The Human Perspective

George Miller, in an article published in 1964 explaining the nature of psycholinguistics, at one point defines it: "Psycholinguistics deals . . . with the practices that grow out of the biological nature of man and the linguistic capacities of human infants." What is important about this statement is that it too deals with language as part of a biological system —human nature. However, it is a nature quite different from that described by earlier scientific linguists. The consequence for reading theory and instruction is that a new light now clarifies a variety of traditional practices and just good hunches about children's learning and the how and why of reading instruction.

Most important, the idea that what we are is a product of external conditioning or environmental manipulation is clearly contradicted. We have a nature, an animal/human nature. Our animal/human characteristics are highly different from most other animals. This does not make us any less natural creatures. Psycholinguistics concentrates our attention on the nature of this uniqueness.

The psycholinguists hone in on the human mind and its search for meaning. Here is where man's uniqueness finds its paradigmatic expression. From the time of the year-old child's holophrastic (one-word) sentence, the questioning and search for order, structure, and meaning define the workings of this young mind. Language is the preeminent vehicle in this search. It is a process that flowers from inward outward like a growing, then blossoming rose.

The psycholinguists like to emphasize that the basic unit

of language is the sentence. Naturally, it starts with recognition of the word in learning and reading. The word is what is called a lexical unit, a unit of meaning. However, the word alone is ambiguous. It needs the association of syntactical order (words in a sentence) and phonemic nuances (recognized sounds) in a particular language to give a total grammatical effect of precise meaning.

An adult knows and uses between 10^4 and 10^5 words (10,000 and 100,000). From these words, humans can produce at least 10^{20} sentences. To speak all the possible twenty-word sentences that humans could produce from their personal experience would take 100,000,000 centuries. No conditioner from the outside could conceivably cause to have "chained" that kind of stimulus-response behavior in the individual. (Miller, 1964) Nagy and Anderson (1984) estimate that middle grade readers might encounter between 10^5 and 10^6 (100,000 and 1,000,000) or more words in their yearly reading experience.

All languages have between twenty and fifty phonemes, those units of sound mentioned above that languages build into their spoken systems. (Yet to be explained is why all human groups need to use this twenty-to-fifty span of different sounds for their languages.) The dot and dash of Morse code could be thought of as two phonemes. We can build an alphabet out of these two phonemes and still communicate ideas. All languages have systems of grammar to help organize these sensory sound-making aspects into a meaningful whole.

Because there are many other symbolic structures that convey meaning—such as in mathematics and music—we now realize that language is only a facilitator to acquire knowledge and meaning. We say that meaning lies in the deep structure of the brain, such that when we truly understand something we rarely lose it. It may be difficult to recover this knowledge. Sometimes psychoanalysts are good for this process. Others use a diary.

Very young children seem to understand language before they can express their own meanings verbally. This argues that human speech and action probably trigger an innate receptivity to language and its function to construct order in meaning. Why it is that we understand and can produce so vast an amount of verbal material that we have not encountered before, we do not know. All of us speak sentences every day that we have never before heard or uttered.

We have been able to identify several discrete language areas in the brain that coordinate the facilitation of thought. Yet it is still unclear how our deepest forms of thinking work both with language and without it. Thought in mathematics, music, the visual world of ordinary experience, and in a wide variety of human activities expresses itself without the developed use of traditional language skills.

The brain and its language areas, so different from any other communicating guidance system in animals, seem to have grown in tandem. The language system of humans is part of the cerebral cortex, the thinking part of the brain. The chimpanzee, by contrast, has its call system of vocalizations located, as do other animals, in the limbic system, the lower mammalian part of the brain. Such a great difference in brain structure and communication function points to the probable fact that the separation of our genus *Homo* from the other anthropoids took place many millions of years ago. Human language and its various derivatives—speech, reading and writing—are indeed marvelously unique creations of nature.

Reading in a Language

We can ask the question then: If the spoken language is such an ancient, unique, and truly natural capacity of the human race, if spoken language is found universally among the peoples of our world, how can we explain the relative rarity of writing and reading up until the twentieth century? Further, what is the relationship of writing to speaking, or reading to listening? The answer from psycholinguistics is that what we are observing in these four different behavior skills —writing, speaking, reading, and listening—are all aspects of language use.

We can disagree with the behaviorists and their reading theorists, the phonics/linguistics people. Reading is *not* "written-down speech." The above language forms are all means by which we communicate or absorb meaning. They are each equally vehicles of communication and not necessarily dependent on one another. The title of an important book edited by James F. Kavanagh and Ignatius G. Mattingly states it: *Language By Ear and By Eye.* Language by ear is the natural language rooted in the brain and facilitated by a unique thick tongue freely moving from its roots in a relatively simply structured supralaryngeal area in back of the throat. The simply structured human pharynx and the thick mobile tongue together with the language areas of the brain have been coordinately evolved in humans alone to serve the speech function.

Writing and reading capability are indeed historically rooted in their creation to the natural spoken language by the fact that they are preceded by the spoken version and often roughly coordinated with it. In the second chapter, we described the early pictographic versions of language of Sumeria and Egypt. Neither had any phonemic (sound) content. Again, the logographs of the Chinese are the purely semantic written form, independent of the spoken language, so much so that the various spoken vernaculars of the different geographical areas are mutually unintelligible, even though students from all parts of China can learn to read and understand the same classical Mandarin written forms.

We have also experienced in various language pathologies (aphasia) how one or more aspects of language use can be lost without affecting the others, and most important, without destroying the deeper intellectual capacity of the individual, though its expression may be hindered. Sometimes these language deficits are amazingly specific in their odd inhibitions, sometimes destroying the use of discrete parts of speech, testifying to the fact that the brain and its language compatability constitute a mosaic of skills and functions that are coordinated by the larger organization of the nervous system.

The problem of reading as it is laid out by psycholinguistics is to find the specific internal and individual maturational processes that will assist the child in finding the natural means to translate the visual symbols of written language into meaning. This does not mean that we are involved in a purely visual linguistic process. The fact that deaf children are so seriously wounded in their language abilities and that this deficit seriously inhibits their potential reading abilities argues for a close relationship between natural language development—hearing and speaking—and the subsequent more abstract and learned skills of reading and writing.

Above all, two ideas strike us as central to understanding the reading revolution that is overtaking the disciplines. The first is that learning to read is a subset skill of a more general language development. The second is that language in general, with reading and writing as elements in the process, is a vehicle for a more basic human characteristic—the acquisition and communication of meaning. Reading is not word calling, i.e., decoding the written visual material to its verbal auditory equivalent. It is part of the process of acquiring knowledge, of organizing it in terms of a deep structure of experimental and symbolic understandings, all made possible by the quintessentially human organ, the cortical brain.

FURTHER READING

Chomsky, N. (1959) "Review of Verbal behavior," by B. F. Skinner. *Language.* Vol. 35, 26-58.

Goodman, K. (1976) "Reading: a psycholinguistic guessing game," in H. Singer and R. Ruddell, eds. *Theoretical models and processes of reading,* 2nd ed. Newark, Del.: International Reading Association.

Kavanagh, J. F. and I. G. Mattingly, eds. (1972) *Language by ear and by eye.* Cambridge, Mass.: MIT Press.

Miller, George A. (1964) "The psychologists." *Encounter,* Vol. 23, 1, 29-37.

Miller, George A. (1977) *Spontaneous apprentices: Children and language.* New York: Seabury.

Nagy, W. E. and R. C. Anderson. (1984) "How many words are there in printed school English." *Reading Research Quarterly,* Spring, 304-330.

Skinner, B. F. (1957) *Verbal behavior.* New York: Appleton, Century, Crofts.

Vygotsky, L. S. (1962) *Thought and language.* Cambridge, Mass.: MIT Press.

Walcutt, Charles et al. (1974) *Teaching reading, a phonic/linguistic approach to developmental reading.* New York: Macmillan.

PART II

The Reading Process

5

The Child
and Readiness

Do We Need Kindergarten?

T HERE IS A magical moment in reading. For most children, it happens sometime after the sixth birthday, almost always before the seventh. For centuries in Europe, reading instruction began after the child turned seven. It was an intuitive recognition of a natural maturing point, a time the process of learning to read had a good chance of success.

Here in the United States, intuition and tradition were not enough. We Americans of scientific and experimental mind had to know more definitely, why and when. Thus, in the 1920's, research was focused on the problem, and indeed revealed a general time for success in actual reading instruction. The pedagogical norm was struck. Carleton Washburn, a progressive superintendent in suburban Winnetka, Illinois, and William Gray, Dean of the University of Chicago School of Education and an authority in psychology and reading, set the moment of readiness at six-and-one-half years of age. For a half century, teachers obeyed the dictum: Delay actual reading instruction, as distinct from readiness preparation, until the children had matured biosocially, and for the great majority this would occur by the age of 6.5.

What then were we to do for the earlier years? The tradition of the kindergarten was well established in the United States by the twenties. However, it was clear that finger painting, block building, choral chanting, seesaws and swings were not enough of an educational rationale to induce the financial community fathers to proffer tax support for classrooms of mere play. Gradually the readiness movement took hold. The early years were to be a preparation for schooling, without the imposition of systematic instruction.

This was not effected without a measure of controversy and discussion both within and without the profession. The reason for controversy was simple. There seemed to be little cause-and-effect relationship between the experiencing of a preschool and kindergarten readiness program and a child's automatically achieved reading or other school success. Just as often a child tossed into first grade without benefit of any preparatory classroom exposure would start reading like a house afire. Others having their full measure of early years' schooling would stumble through the crucial age period in first and second grade and yet seem to be interminably plagued with reading difficulties.

School boards were quick to note this in their attempts to curb school expense growth and to limit the tax bite for local citizens. Thus the question of the effectiveness of these preschool programs was never clearly resolved, even though we understood the significance of the crucial transitional period (6.5) in a child's intellectual growth.

If reading was like any other intellectual or, even more broadly, learning skill, shouldn't the teaching and discipline of its elements help those who were subject to the exposure,

as compared to those untrained and uninitiated? Tha
the central question that psycholinguistics had to answer, ir
only to support a general theory of what reading was and
how it might better be taught both to young and old.

The Three Systems of Reading

The question thus focuses on the special nature of that
skill we call reading. To be honest, we must admit that mere
exposure to broad-based learning experiences in preschool
and kindergarten does not guarantee future reading success.
Thus let us pause and without further ado present for consideration the beginning of an explanation of this baffling fact.
Three elements in the child's mental structure contribute to
the entire process of reading competency. It should be emphasized that these elements are still only vaguely and generally understood. However, it is a basis of knowledge for more
study and research. This is where we now stand. From this
perspective we build our proposals for teaching reading.
When new knowledge is produced that changes our understanding of the elements and relationships of human perception and thought, then our view of the reading process, pedagogy, and curriculum development will likewise be altered.
We must be ever open to the new, ready to drop the comfortable but antiquated beliefs that we hold onto as if our life
depends upon them. It doesn't.

The model: (1) **The sensory system.** The child receives
information about the outside world through the five senses.
Some senses are more important as transmitters of information than others. Obviously, for the natural language, hearing is crucial. We know, for example, that for deaf children
even a tiny bit of auditory information can bring about a
great improvement in language ability. Obviously children

are quite different in how they react to the same minimum amount of residual hearing. Of course the profoundly deaf child who can be contacted only visually or tactilely with regard to language—written—operates under a tragically heavy deficit.

Note how the blind child able to learn to speak can rapidly be taught to read through Braille or else through listening to talking-book records, for example. The sensory system then is a necessary precondition to language and reading ability. But it is not sufficient. This is because the sensory system is "intellectually blind" without the other two dimensions. These latter are necessary to make sense of the purely physical vibration of sound or the corpuscles of light that these main distance sense receptors are capable of pulling in.

(2) **The integrational system.** This is the most mysterious and unexplored dimension of the learning/language reading process. It is a complex of skills that lies between the pure sensory input and the final cognitive understanding of things. The integrational system itself encompasses language ability which, I should warn the reader here, does not exhaust nor is it synonymous with intelligence, cognition, and thought. One can be highly intelligent and able without using language, speech, or reading with any degree of skill. Great chess players and mathematicians are examples. Perhaps one of the most supreme minds of all time, Mozart, used his language skills very casually, scattering insightful, analytical letters with the most primitive of scatalogical references. Yet this man had a mind of such power, fluency, and spontaneous creativity (he had been musically educated with great care) that specialized education in langauge expression might even have impeded his flow of thought.

The key to understanding the integrative system is to view it as connected with both systems on either end—sensory and semantic—as a transmitter, but wired in a highly complex set of hierarchies. The most intelligent often have systems breakdowns in their neurological "wiring," in reading, called "specific dyslexia."

(3) **The semantic system.** This is where human understanding occurs. It is still clouded in mystery and controversy, yet certain factors in human cognition can be set forth with a measure of certainty. When we truly learn something, i.e., the relationship and organization of experience—intellectual or commonsense—it remains in our long-term memory as long as we live. Yes, we often have to find the means, the trigger that will release it from memory. But the key to all understanding is our ability to work out cause-and-effect relationships, to subject new experiences to principles so that we can operate in a human world that is without fixed biological instincts.

Many psychologists called the locus of human intelligence "g" after the work of the early twentieth-century English psychologist, Charles Spearman. "G" stands for a general principle out of which our various skills and aptitudes take on substance. Language use and the ability to read become real for a child to the point that they release understanding. There are many children who can hear and see, whose sensory systems are intact, who have workable integrational systems, whose hearing, seeing, and tactile skills work "in synch," yet who are what teachers call "word callers." Simply, they do not understand what they are reading.

Often their inner intelligence, "g", is not up to comprehending the meaning of what they are reading. It is a rare "good" reader who will not meet his or her semantic master when confronting unfamiliar or difficult reading material. The causes are various, educational or intellectual, to name two.

However, it is likewise a rare authority on educational, psychological, or philosophical matters who will not concede that we all differ in a rough quantitative way in our ability to master various intellectually demanding ideas, linguistic or not. One way of expressing the concept of "g" quantitatively is the I.Q. score. Even if one is suspicious of I.Q. numbers as a real standard of evaluation of intelligence, rational people will admit to the reality of variable intelligence between individuals. There are also few authorities who would not concede that individuals who seem to be of nearly the same intellectual ability may have distinctly different aptitudes and talents. Here is where the concept of the integrational system (system 2) complements the other two levels, especially the semantic system. For, a mere bit of sensory information can go miles in releasing the two systems—integrational (system 2) and semantic (system 3)—for use. Yet, what is an "idiot savant" if not an individual with enormous linguistic, mathematical, musical, or artistic powers that utilize either rote memory or a few rigidly mechanical associative processes. All of these are what we might call surface-structure skills, allied generally with the integrational domain. These people don't really think relationally.

Preparing the Child to Read

Let us begin with the fact that reading or even working with numbers is an abstract process. Children do not automatically understand the meaning of written symbols as they do the meaning of spoken words in their mother language. In the latter the process is natural and inevitable for a child who can hear and who is whole. In contrast with our visual world of natural understandings—trees, houses, clouds, faces, smiles—the coming together of letters in sequence constitutes a whole new visual/mental semantic. Indeed, here at least two different parts of the brain are involved.

An experiment was done in the 1950's in which subjects were asked to wear glasses with specially devised lenses wherein the world was turned upside down. In a few days, the subjects made a mental readjustment out of the visual sensory/integrational systems. The mind and understanding turned all the visual images right side up. There was one exception. The visual integrational systems for reading could not be so easily reversed. Why?

Children must gradually learn that certain marks—lines, circles—stand for another set of meanings in the world. This is in addition to the voices that they hear, the things they see, touch, or smell. Mothers read to children, show them books, point out signs in the street, even logos—McDonalds, Coca-Cola, Ford.

The idea is born in the child's mind even while these marks are still "mysterious" that they have a special brand of meaning. Books, magazines, newspapers at home reinforce the expectation in the young two-to-four-year-old child that there is a world of interesting things denoted by this "written stuff," especially with the pictures that help tell the story. But the reading (integrational) systems are visually still too immature for educators to do more than help the child trace simple shapes or recognize letters and the sounds they stand for.

Eleanor Gibson has done research that reveals a growing awareness in the child of the special nature of these written marks—the budding capacity to copy shapes, to recognize differences in letters, and to relate them to clearly enunciated sounds and common words. As the child approaches age four, this becomes even more evident and nears a period where so-called readiness instruction can systematically heighten his/her consciousness to the elements in the language/learning process that involve writing and reading.

In the ferment of the late sixties and early seventies there was much concern to avoid the reading disabilities that were then beginning to be recognized in the process of reading instruction. It was thought that readiness could both screen out potential problems as well as institute therapies to modify probable disabilities before they seriously handicapped the child. People like Klaus Weddel and Anna Gillingham, taking some of their suggestions from the earlier work of Maria Montessori with Italian pauper children, concentrated on the perceptual/motor factor in learning.

Perceptual/motor programs stressed the comparative developmental rates of young children as they gained independence of arm and leg movement, learned to walk a straight line, a circle, to distinguish left-right, up-down etc. The logical argument was that such reading disability predictivity could not begin before letter and word recognition skills came into place, i.e., between five and six years of age. However, some of these perceptual motor (P/M) developmental difficulties could be remediated at an earlier stage. Any great deviation from the P/M norm thus would have some predictive validity in terms of confronting reading difficulties that would show themselves later on. Thus, work on P/M development was the recommendation.

The movement developed some professional visibility during this period, but it gradually lost its impact when it became evident that many nicely coordinated children never learned to read, and that many painfully awkward children, like the ones we sometimes describe as having "two left feet," learned to read with great speed when their time came. Clearly the P/M factors in neurological maturation worked off other independent (integrational?) structures of the brain as compared with written language.

Even popular reading readiness tests such as the *Metropolitan*, published by Harcourt Brace Jovanovich, sent a mixed message. The test has a number of parts: (1) picture recognition, (2) picture story-meaning completion, (3) geometric shape recognition, (4) letter/sound recognition, (5) number knowledge, (6) "draw a man." To the uninitiated it would seem clear that the letter and geometric shape recognition parts of the test would have some predictability since the test was given at the end of kindergarten (age 5.5) or the beginning of first grade (age 6.0). Oddly enough, it was the purely semantic, intellectual number recognition test that predicted the future "good" or "poor" reader better than the others, though the predictability was not exceptionally high. (Hildreth)

The reason for this seemingly anomalous fact lies in the nature of the long-run reading process. What we call fluent reading, to be described in detail in Chapter 8, involves a rapid movement beyond the visual language systems to the semantic system. To be a good reader, one must quickly code the visual marks to meaning. Those children who in kindergarten are able to abstract relational meaning on the readiness tests are more likely to be able to go directly to "deep-structure" semantic indentification unless there is a rare and unique specific reading disorder that affects letter and word recognition (the integrational system) and at the same time does not touch number recognition and number relationships (which we think work off other parts of the integrational system of the brain).

What this argues for in the relationship between readiness training and reading is that the accomplishment of reading is most efficiently achieved by stressing those skills that are the closest to the actual process of reading, namely: letter-sound knowledge, acquaintance with and practice in distinguishing and writing numbers and letters relating to words and concepts. Also, the development in the child of a whole series of understandings with regard to the structure of stories —characters, alternative endings, questions about personalities, sequences of events in stories—act to flesh out a child's comprehension as to how the world works.

As the reader here knows, reading is a process of extracting meaning. The sound and shape of words and sentences are relevant to knowledge if they release meaningful ideas to the child. Often, the seemingly most intelligent child can't learn to read. Such a child may have problems of determining sight-to-sound equivalences or of stabilizing the spatial sequence of letters to make words. Even moving across the page may be difficult. The integrational system is either not yet neurologically matured in the child, or else there are serious congenital, either hereditary or acquired, blockages, that need to be identified. These can possibly be bypassed with specialized instruction that helps the child get beyond the sensory inputs to the deeper structured semantic level through alternate learning pathways.

In other cases, as in the intriguing example of early readers, we find a precocity in the maturation of the reading system that often extends beyond the intellectual maturity of the child. The work of Dolores Durkin is crucial here. She shows that early readers, those from 3.5 to 5.5 years of age, vary considerably in intelligence. What they have in common is a highly matured integrational system that allows them to take a few phonetic clues, the sounds of letters and words, make a series of inductive jumps from sound to sight of letters and words, develop an inner neurological dictionary of these relationships, and decode new sight words to their equivalent sounds. Soon they are going directly from the visual marks to the recognition of short sentence meanings.

Many young fluent readers surprise us in their early ability to go directly to the semantic level. They also often reveal their special talents by the peculiar errors they make in their oral reading. A child will orally read a sentence written, for instance, "Jack and Jill went up the hill to fetch a pail of water" as "Jack and Jill *ran* up the hill to *fill* a *bucket* of water," substituting one or several of the words italicized.

The exact words the child has read are different, but the meaning remains essentially the same. Kenneth Goodman has labeled this kind of error a "miscue," that is, not a substantive error of meaning but a minor miscue created when the child doesn't give enough *visual* attention to the material. Why would a child make such an error in the first place?

Frank Smith, in *Understanding Reading*, has described the process of fluent reading (reading for meaning) as "predicting" the way through the written material. If a person visually focuses on every letter and word, inevitably there is a slowing up in the amount of written material that the eye and the mind can grasp.

What happens is that the digestion of this material in short-term memory is blocked before the child can get the gist of things semantically. (We will discuss this process more fully later on.) Natural readers realize that unless they move rapidly over the reading page, they will become intellectually constipated and suffer memory breakdown, so they whiz along getting the meaning of the sentence, though occasionally missing on some of the words. They assume "run" for "went," or "fill" for "fetch," or "bucket" for "pail." They were wrong because they did not consistently check their guesses visually. The meaning was essentially right, of course, for those words are semantically roughly synonymous.

Frank Smith calls this predicting one's way through the material. This means the child is guessing at the written marks so that he/she does not have to slow down and foul up enjoyment of the ideas. This is what reading should be. For a young reader, the modest price of those erroneous predictions, miscues leads him/her into making those innocuous but importantly revealing errors in the process of reading orally.

Another example of early reading that throws light on the challenge of readiness programs is given in the work of Jane Torrey (Connecticut College) with a black child of working-class parents in Atlanta, Georgia. This four-year-old child, John, developed precocious reading skills by watching television. He noted the spoken words of the advertisements, which were often followed by their written equivalents. Having had a few clues from parents as to the basic sounds of several of the letters, he was able to go on from that idea—spoken sound-written letter sound—to make a series of inductive generalizations about the relationship of the spoken form to the written world of ideas to which he was being exposed. Since there were magazines, newspapers, and books in the home he had time to peruse them at his leisure, to figure out their meanings from what he had learned via the T.V.

John's family was stable, both parents worked. The home had a number of middle-class advantages. John spoke with the heavy local Black Atlanta English, yet this caused him no difficulty in translating New York T.V. English into his reading repertoire, both oral and silent. He did tend to write in his own spoken dialect.

What is especially interesting is that, developing his skill practically alone, he outpaced his older siblings, who were already in school. In terms of tested intelligence, however, John was only average for his age. In fact, his general academic progress revealed a not exceptional student. Why was this?

It is Dolores Durkin's more general research with early readers that helps us to understand the seeming anomaly of John's early reading. Early readers are to be found at all points of the intellectual spectrum, from slow-to-average to extremely bright youngsters. Very bright early readers lose their advantage over very bright late readers somewhere around second or third grade. On the other hand, average intelligent early readers maintain their advantage over average intelligent late readers.

What this seems to indicate is that the purely reading/language skills—decoding from sight to sound, being able to read rapidly and fluently for meaning—are skills that can be placed in the so-called integrational area—coordinating visual-auditory skills—neurologically. The point of the distinction between the integrational and the semantic or intellectual domain is that each seems to function as a separate entity. The ripening of one is not necessarily determined by the other. In many respects, each is an independent factor in the development of reading ability.

The Purpose of Readiness

It is true that, on the average, children begin to read before the age of six-and-one-half. What matters is maturation. The reader may ask, maturation of what? After all, these are young children. Certainly reading ability has little to do with those sensory/motor coordination skills that we know to be so variable in the developmental rates of children. Personality maturation would likewise be a poor guide for predicting reading success.

Yes, it is true that the female matures earlier in all phases of development, including reading. However, even among girls, one cannot make sure predictions about reading from psychological or personality evidence. As we will discuss later in greater detail, all evidence points directly to the so-called integrational areas of learning—between the reception of percepts by the sensory organs and the ultimate transferral of information into the semantic level, or deep structure. The key to early reading success lies in this midrange of psychoneurological brain organization.

It is here that the ability to process visual and auditory information so that it is rapidly turned into meaning takes place. For various individually discrete reasons, each child has his/her internal timetable for success. Teachers must be sensitive and aware of these rhythms in the development of every child. Even the most intelligent child of 6.5 years of age might not yet be ready neurologically (integrational system) to read fluently. A program of readiness experiences will smooth the way for all children so that when the time for reading arrives, it can occur with the least trauma and the greatest chance for success.

There is much indirect teaching that can prepare the child both intellectually and emotionally for the coming of that crucial first step. This is where readiness experiences can help, especially in the parental and familial environment for learning. Invariably, learning anything well is a matter of will. Children who have been abused or subjected to unremitting scholastic pressure or for any number of other reasons, can shut their minds or stiffen their backs. They can say "nothing doing" without using a single word.

On the other hand, drop a child into first grade, expose him to some simple books, and with a minimum of instruction he/she will often start to read. That is why, as we noted earlier, the Europeans tended to delay reading until age seven. They would have nothing to do with the coddling protectiveness of our child-oriented society. And for the relatively small percentage of students who went to school in traditional European society, this worked well enough.

Finally there is another rationale for having a highly articulated readiness program today. Modern society demands universal literacy. Given our growing knowledge of the depth and incidence of reading disabilities, plus the astounding rate of illiteracy, suffered especially by males, the potential diagnostic role of readiness programs appears increasingly vital.

In the old days, teachers talked about the casual relationship of emotional problems in children to subsequent learning disabilities. Well, it turned out that many emotionally disturbed children read furiously—for escape?—and many seemingly well-adjusted children couldn't or wouldn't learn to read. Today, we acknowledge the fact that not learning to read is such a stigma that a subsequent emotional upset is virtually assured. It is most urgent that we act to interdict such reading failures before they occur by identifying the potential victims.

It was for these same reasons that the French government in 1905 asked Alfred Binet to devise a test of intelligence that could predict subsequent school failure. We need readiness programs to predict potential reading problems. It is essential that we remember that reading failure is not necessarily the failure of the intellectual system of the child. Quite the contrary, reading works off the delicate, complex, yet mysterious connective circuitry (integrational system) that really defines our various individual aptitudes and incompetencies. Some of the most brilliant people in history have had reading problems. Perhaps the delicacy of this skill explains why reading came so late and variably in the evolution of human culture and civilization.

FURTHER READINGS

Bradley, L. and P. E. Bryant. (1983) "Categorizing sounds and learning to read—a causal connection." *Nature,* Vol. 301, 419-421.

Durkin, D. (1966) *Children who read early.* New York: Teachers College Press.

Gates, Arthur I. (1937) "The necessary mental age for beginning reading." *Elementary School Journal.* Vol. 37, 497-508.

Gibson, Eleanor J. (1965) "Learning to read." *Science.* Vol. 148, 1066-1072.

Gibson, Eleanor J. (1970) "The ontogeny of reading." *American Psychologist.* Vol. 25, 136-142.

Gillingham, A. and B. W. Stillman. (1966) *Remedial training for children with specific difficulties in reading, spelling and phonetics.* Cambridge, Mass.: Educators Publishing Service.

Hildreth, Gertrude. (1950) *Readiness for school beginners.* New York: Harcourt Brace.

Torrey, Jane W. (1969) "Learning to read without a teacher: A case study." *Elementary English.* Vol. 46, 550-556.

Washburne, C. and M. Morphett. (1931) "When should children begin to read." *Elementary School Journal.* Vol. 31, 496-503.

Wedell, Klaus. (1970) "Perceptuo-motor factors." *Journal of Special Education.* Vol. 4, 3.

6

Mediated Reading

The Meaning of Phonics

MEDIATED READING IS a concept describing a stage in the process of learning to read that is fraught with controversy. It designates the stage that follows reading readiness. It is the stage before "true" reading, described in the following chapter. So far, so good, no controversy. The controversy lies in the claim that mediated reading is the stage usually absorbed into phonics teaching.

Ostensibly one teaching young children to read through the phonics method is teaching true reading. Phonics is overlain today with a haze of pseudo-certainty that a particular kind of decoding of printed material to sound, thus to the natural language, then to understanding, constitutes reading. As we will show, this is untrue. More of that later. Now let us stake our own claim.

When is a child ready to read? Answer: when the readiness program, as determined by diverse maturational tests, establishes that a child can distinguish letter shapes, can make some inductive sound generalizations from various letters, can even distinguish and name the sounds of the letter elements of simple words. Naturally a child must be able to hear sound differences in letter and word pronunciation, although even here some children with poor auditory discrimination of sound elements (phonemes), thus with only minimal phonetic skills, can go straight to the written text and read for meaning. These children kept the sight method of teaching reading alive for decades. Unfortunately, percentage-wise, they are probably a diminishing group among our youthful readers.

The child entering first grade is about six years of age. According to our previously noted reading chronology, most children should be reading by age seven, with the average at about 6.5. In theory, this gives the first grade teacher four to six months, from September to March, to move the children over the line into reading. During these months, much remedial readiness is meted out to those students who arrive in class without the school or home background that prepares them for systematic reading instruction.

A reflection of the increasing importance of such readiness training in first grade, as compared with the past, is the simplification of basal reader instruction. Today, there seems to be an infinite number of preprimers involving the minute progression and sequencing of skill training in the basic readiness areas of letter-sound awareness and letter-shape differences. Even skills such as following directions, habituating eye movements, and basic spoken verbal comprehension are now part of the first grade curriculum. In the 1930's, first grade was much more a time of actual reading instruction.

In the days of the look-say method, these early months of first grade were devoted to teaching the shapes and distinctive visual elements of a core sight vocabulary of words and sentences out of which more fluent reading was supposed to grow by the second grade. The phonic elements, for reasons alluded to earlier in this book, were felt to be restrictive and redundant. In most schools, however, practical experience dictated that some phonics instruction was essential. Thus the teaching of reading throughout the United States between 1920 and 1950 was more eclectic than the professional leadership supposed.

Through mediated reading the child is acquainted with the visual-letter-word equivalents of his/her natural language. Since the normal six-year-old child understands and speaks the language clearly and articulately, the problem is to decode to sound the mysterious marks on the page. The many rules that constitute systematic or explicit phonics teaching supposedly help the child in encountering new combinations of letters and applying these rules in decoding to the natural language sound equivalents, subsequently understanding the meaning of the written material.

It is probably fair to say that even a linguistically/visually precocious child goes through a mediated reading stage. This child would need little overt instruction in sound-letter-word equivalents to break the code and whiz through a sentence. Still the letters must be put into words. The words must be assembled visually and rapidly into sentences and thus understood. This takes even the most precocious some time. Classroom reading instruction is usually necessary for identifying the words, finding their meaning, then extracting the meaning spontaneously through the visual sentence scanning process.

Today, the overwhelming need for mediated reading instruction in the school population necessitates a different kind of approach by educators. Most children who need such help have a slower maturing linguistic/visual processing system (integrational stage). They need much help in decoding the letter and word images into sound equivalents. The child is already beyond the rudimentary readiness skills of letter/symbol recognition and sound differences distillation, yet not matured enough to encode spontaneously the visual image into meaning. There is good reason here for the child to be intellectually frustrated.

If we use the perceptual psychologist's terminology, children need the help of their short-term memory to hold together the two, three, or four items perceived (letter combinations of, for example, ba/by, fa/th/er) long enough to combine them into meaning. If this process can truly be called fluent reading and if long-term memory is thought of as the ultimate receptacle of meaning and comprehension, then short-term memory becomes the great assister, even the crutch of the mediated reader. For, short-term memory keeps the letter elements in the mind so as to form the word, and the three or four words to form a simple sentence.

The tragedy for so many readers was the return to systematic (explicit) phonics instruction over the past generation. Such readers were often unable to go beyond the frustratingly slow pace of decoding to sound, often suffering short-term memory breakdown. Word or sentence meaning becomes evanescent after three or four seconds of "sounding out" and because of the turgid pace of their reading, comprehension was lost. Our recent pedagogical failures lie in the simple fact that we transformed what is in reality a brief moment in the scholastic evolution of the child (mediated reading) into an eternal precept.

The reason for this egregious error was the profession's timid reaction to those politicized attacks during the reading wars that effectively dumped the young learner out of the look-say "pan" into the phonics "fire." A generation of crippled readers has been the result.

The Alphabet as Cause

The problem of beginning, or mediated, reading, at least in the English-speaking countries, to an extent in other western nations also, lies in the nature of our system of writing.

The alphabet as applied to our spoken system of English is a hodgepodge of centuries of accumulation. The result is that the spoken system has an enormous number of written variations. The spelled version of our sounds often doesn't hold true—Ex: *father, fathead; alphabet, alfalfa; nation, neighbor.*

We are stuck with an alphabetic form of writing for good or ill. Probably it is good, until our population and the others around the world become linguistic prodigies. For, the Chinese who have perhaps the most abstract and intellectually most economical form of writing—in that it approaches pure semantics (no phonetics) and incorporates little syntactics—are turning toward our model. They are no longer intent on the exclusivity of the Confucian scholar or civil service model of culture. Universal literacy is a Communist goal, and thus an alphabetic alternative is gradually being introduced.

The value of the alphabet for writing and reading is that it demands less both from the intellect and the memory. Unlike the Chinese logographic system, which is made up of thousands of graphemes, all standing for words (meanings), our system requires the learning of only twenty-six different units. Out of these units of "sound," we construct a language in which spelling attempts to mirror the spoken version. The problem is that the spoken aspect of language itself changes over time. It is clear that, evolving over a period of some 2,000 years, written language in its alphabetic form constitutes a brilliant compromise between the abstract demands of writing for meaning and the necessities for simplicity, communicability, and remaining close visually to the natural spoken language. The latter helps serve the purpose of universal literacy.

One way that we can appreciate the English-speaking child's dilemma in learning to read is to contrast it with the Chinese equivalent. The latter, or his Japanese confrere learning the classical Kanji script, must first learn thousands of subtly different visual symbols that stand for word-meanings. With these, the child learns a series of semantic modifiers and marks (plural-singular, gender, past-present) which can be applied to the basic logograph. Because these symbols have no fixed sound equivalent in their written expression, oral reading in the various geographies of China produces mutually incomprehensible expression.

This could eventually take place in the United States between north and south, east and west. However, the alphabet, which roughly represents certain traditional sounds, holds things together enough to maintain a modest compatibility. Mass communication has helped in no little manner. In China, the young student faces quite an intellectual task right at the start. In addition, the purely visual sequence of decoding to meaning presents a problem to Chinese predisposed to a certain kind of specific reading disability. They have absolutely no step-by-step sound-grammar to help them as they move slowly along the columns.

As a matter of fact, the Japanese scholar Kiyoshi Makita has noted that even excluding those kinds of integrational level disabilities, failure in reading classical Kanji is immediately seen with the slow learner. There are few children in the United States who could not learn to read on a rudimentary level because of merely below-average intelligence. It may be a slow process, yet a glimmer of understanding and achievement can be attained; most such students can break the usual alphabetic code by simple translation of the visual symbol into sound.

Among the Japanese, and presumably the Chinese and Koreans also, the average and below-average scholar would have great difficulty mastering the written language. The initial hurdle is high. Interestingly, among the northeastern Asiatic population, the intelligence levels seem to be on average extremely high. Thus in theory difficulties in reading such scripts might not be daunting for the great majority of Orientals. Yet the educational expenditure, even given the real efficiency of the written language, separated as it has been from the local spoken vernacular, still renders classical Chinese probably too esoteric for our dynamic era.

Letters and Sounds

The problem in building up a written language alphabetically lies in choosing from the various sounds of the spoken language and identifying them, then symbolizing them in writing. Fortunately or not, written languages evolved before sophisticated linguistic analysis created the concept of the *phoneme.* The Japanese Kana alphabet is perhaps the only widely used written form that consciously attempts to reflect the spoken language.

To make itself communicable every spoken language has to "choose" from the almost infinite number of possible sounds—"phones"—those "phonemes" that will be used in its particular culture. Almost all languages identify and use between twenty and fifty such sounds out of which the spoken language becomes functional. Using the dot—dash of the Morse code as examples of two phonemes that are combined to form a communication medium, we can see how flexible such a system can be. Too many phonemes and the language becomes over-complex, acoustically overly concrete. Too few phonemes leave too much to interpretation. The Morse code has to have special communication facilitators—light flashes or auditory clicks—that our vocal apparatus could not match in specificity. A Morse code language might in addition be a slow medium of expression. We might experience frequent S.T.M. (short-term memory) breakdowns. Thus, most languages wind up with close to fifty phonemes. The Japanese Kana has forty-six, our C.B.S. television version of English about forty-four.

Oddly enough, since our own *written* language as it has evolved has only twenty-six letters, we must create many ad hoc combinations of letters: "ch," "oo," "ou," allow for multiple letter uses: "k," "ck," "c," in which different letters stand for the same sound; or create different phonemes from the same letter: *apple, ate, eagle, alter.* The mass media have probably slowed down the traditional centrifugal evolution of the spoken language. It makes no sense, as some have suggested, to restructure our writing to reflect speech conventions more accurately. It would also wreak havoc with our historical record. Note the expressions of concern from those who abhor the translation of the King James version of the Bible into modern English.

As we will point out later, the Initial Teaching Alphabet, which has an alphabet of forty-four graphemes, would work like Japanese Kana. It would probably help many reading-disabled children who need the phonics support that slow visual reading makes necessary. In the end, however, such an extended alphabet would break too radically with the past and present its own special difficulties for the future.

We probably will have to cope with our alphabetic system. However, it does raise the special problem of teaching in the so-called mediated stage of reading. We must ask ourselves how it is best surmounted? What are its special difficulties?

Consider the first-grade child just beginning to accumulate a series of phonics principles, exceptions, and special cases. The child must move over the page gradually from left to right recognizing the visual marks, the letters representing single sounds or clusters of sounds. After that, the child will begin first to recognize words, then, at the least, short sentences. It is a slow process in the beginning. Importantly, we must reiterate, comprehension is the key to the attainment of reading competency, as opposed to mouthing or word calling. Often, deceptively, this decoding to sound is called reading. This is where we must consider an important psychoneurological category. Often it is a roadblock to extracting reading comprehension.

Getting Beyond Short-term Memory

The psychoneurological category referred to above is *short-term memory* (S.T.M.). We have alluded to this concept earlier. It is crucial to elaborate here, to explain the relationsip of S.T.M. to the reading process. Logically, it occupies the same position as does the integrational level. In general, it is partway between pure perceptual input and ultimate deep structure of long-term memory comprehension.

Here too we have a tripartite division of labor. First, the sensory information arrives in 1/50th-of-a-second inputs, little bundles of visual information being held in the mind's eye for from 1/5th to 1/2 second. Sensation tumbles after sensation. Usually within this time span, it begins to come together into a structured percept, into some kind of organizational (perceptual) whole.

Second, short-term memory (S.T.M.) enters. Note that we can remember isolated items of thought—telephone numbers, sequences of letters. Call it pure memory in the sense that Cattell's 1885 experiments measured the rate of recall of random letters and words. S.T.M. stands halfway between the sensation perceived by eye, ear, or touch, and the final organization of understanding. It serves to prepare new visual reading material to be related to the pre-existing structure of ideas and concepts that remains indefinitely in the mind's eye. This is the third and ultimate level. We call it long-term memory (L.T.M.).

To understand the problem of reading from the standpoint of S.T.M., think of the child trying to hold a batch of disparate letters and sounds in mind while he/she sorts them out to put them into a meaningful whole. Time is working against the child all the while. For, the child can hold them in mind for only three or four seconds before the S.T.M. is deluged with new sensory perceptions (coming in 1/50th-second gulps) demanding to be organized. What often happens is S.T.M. overload and a consequent short circuit; a memory lapse occurs and the child must start over from the beginning. This is what happens when you try to retain the first telephone number you read from a book as you continue down the column reading more numbers.

The child strives to apply all those learned rules of explicit phonics, correlations of print and sound to the new reading material. Literally a race takes place in the mind between the intellectual recall of phonics rules, their application to the reading material, and the rapid translation of the word into meaning before the visual image itself fades from memory. There can be no comprehension if the child freezes into tunnel vision while straining to apply the rule and does not see enough of the word or sentence. Just as our alphabet requires that the word be stretched out left to right in space, word comprehension requires a perceptive movement of the eyes in space and time. Unless the rules for decoding to sound-meaning come spontaneously, so much time will be needed for the eye and mind to cover the territory on the page that the child will experience S.T.M. overload—new perceptual material crowding out the prior material.

I.T.A.: An Approach to Mediated Reading

One solution to the mediated reading problem is that fascinating beginning reading technique called Initial Teaching Alphabet (I.T.A.). I.T.A. was invented by Sir James Pitman, whose grandfather invented the Pitman shorthand orthography. It consists of forty-four graphemes that attempt to mirror the identifiable phonemes of English.

The usefulness of I.T.A. is that the child has only to learn the sound equivalents of forty-four letters that always sound the same. The many rules and exceptions of traditional orthography (T.O.) are unnecessary. In addition, the tops of letters are identical to those in the T.O. alphabet, so that a child has no difficulty later in making the transition from I.T.A. to T.O. The system was developed this way because, as we will explain later, rapid readers tend to scan only the tops of letters.

For the child in the mediated stage of reading, with a fairly good set of skills in sound discrimination, I.T.A. could be perfect. Here the child has no difficulty with the often bizarre spelling patterns of English. Every word is consistent with the established I.T.A. grapheme sound equivalents so that the child can write whatever he/she can say.

Once the child learns the sound (phoneme) equivalent of each letter (grapheme) he/she doesn't have to learn any more rules. Now the child's eye/mind can move quickly across the page. No more the zillion or so special exceptions, the plethora of phonics rules. All the rules (graphemes, letter combinations) are regular and unchanging. Since we read for meaning, when we have gulped enough visual material for our S.T.M. to organize as a whole, and within the three or four seconds holding limit, we now have a much easier task.

The race through space/time by the child's eye is rewarded with meaning. Like the magic tablet, the S.T.M. slate is now cleared and the child, reinforced by success, moves on to the process of actually enjoying extracting ideas from the mysterious marks on the page. The S.T.M. blockade has here been permanently surmounted.

I.T.A. is not an educational panacea. It has been abandoned by droves of school systems, by teachers who did not want to be burdened with two methods for teaching reading, by school boards who did not want to buy additional and

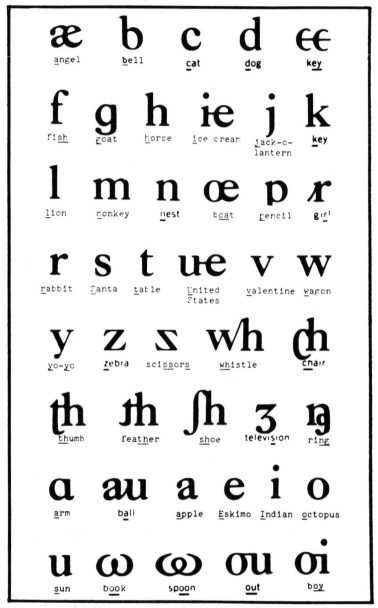

Figure 3   Initial Teaching Alphabet
The Initial Teaching Alphabet orthography and its phonemic equivalents.
(Courtesy the I.T.A. Foundation.)

ie follœd ʃhe tree frog
up in ʃhe tree.
hee jumpt sœ fast
ʃhat ie skinnd mie nee.
did ʃhat stop mee?
œ nœ! ie wonted tω see
ʃhe hous ʃhat ʃhe tree frog
had for mee.

"heer wee ar!" hee sed.
"it iʃ æry and briet,
not a black œld hœl
aʃ dark aʃ ʃhe niet.
yω can see! ʃhær'ʃ a vue!
yω can lωk aull around
at birdʃ in ʃhe skie
and boiʃ on ʃhe ground."

Figure 4   An I.T.A. Story
A first grade "story" that children read in I.T.A. orthography.
(Courtesy the I.T.A. Foundation.)

odd curriculum materials, and finally by parents who did not want to have to learn something new to aid in the education of their children. Also, few today would argue that we ought to regularize our spelling, knowing full well that inevitable changes in the spoken language, the mass media to the contrary, would eventually render any spelling reform null. Thus I.T.A. would always remain a specialized, temporary educational tool.

The pedagogical reading uses of I.T.A. ought to give us pause, for they clearly reflect the status of mediated reading. It was the rare I.T.A. advocate who did not suggest that children should be making the transition to reading in T.O. (traditional orthography) during the second grade. Certainly I.T.A. was to be concluded by the early weeks of grade three, and this was generally viewed as a late conversion. Note, a child could easily make the transition to fluent reading at any stage while still reading in I.T.A. In fact, the point of learning to read in I.T.A. was to assist the child in making the transition from mediated to fluent reading. Obviously the cost of providing advanced reading materials in I.T.A. would have made any delay in such a transition costly. Thus school systems rarely devoted or should devote more than two grades to I.T.A.

Why Mediated Reading?

The mediated reading process ought to be seen as transitional. It is where the child slowly negotiates a process of acquaintance with and extraction of the spoken equivalents of the written symbols. The child learns too to negotiate the material with increasing awareness of the inherent phonics generalizations in the written language. However taught, explicitly or implicitly, these generalizations must be internalized, then spontaneously applied to the reading material. Gradually the child can build up speed in the construction of each word, which leads to the rapid reading of a simple sentence.

All the while, the teacher exposes the child to a wide variety of language experiences—listening, speaking, reading, writing. Eventually, if the mediated stage of reading is handled intelligently, something should happen. One day the child will forget to mouth the sounds, will begin to bypass the hestitant artificial construction of words, and regulate the almost static and often confused eye movements. Then we will see a flexibility and naturalness of attention, much quicker completion of the reading assignments, even a general relaxation of the breathing muscles, perhaps finally a smile at the outcome of a story.

The second phase of reading has here been surmounted; the magic moment has arrived. At what age this occurs varies with the mysteries of individuation. Often, girls will arrive at this point before their male classmates.

The educational question is what classroom curriculum approach will best facilitate a process of transition. Too often, dogmatism and the easy answer substitute for the common practical sense that might extricate us from illusion and lead us back to reality. When one understands the meaning of the next phase in the reading process, it will be impossible for any learned teacher of reading to think that phonics teaching completes the reading cycle.

FURTHER READINGS

Aukerman, R. (1971) *Approaches to beginning reading.* New York: John Wiley.

Chomsky, C. (1976) "After decoding: What?" *Language Arts.* Vol. 53, 288-296; 314.

Durkin, D. (1962) *Phonics and the teaching of reading.* New York: Teachers College Press.

Goodman, K. S. (1976) *Reading: A conversation with Kenneth Goodman.* Glenview, II.: Scott-Foresman.

Makita, Kiyoshi. (1968) "The rarity of reading disabilities in Japanese children." *American Journal of Orthopsychiatry.* Vol. 38, 4, 599-614.

Mazurkiewicz, A. J., ed. (1966) *I. T. A. and the world of English.* Hempstead, N. Y.: I. T. A. Foundation.

Smith, F. (1973) "Decoding: The great fallacy," in *Psycholinguistics and reading.,* ed by F. Smith, Chapter 6, 70-83. New York: Holt, Rinehart, and Winston.

Tzeng, Ovid J. L. and Harry Singer. (1978-1979) "The failure of Steinberg and Yamada to demonstrate superiority of Kanji over Kana for initial reading instruction in Japan." *Reading Research Quarterly,* Vol. 4, 661-667.

Weber, R.M. (1970) "A linguistic analysis of first-grade reading errors." *Reading Research Quarterly,* Vol. 5, 427-451.

7

The Magic Moment

Ancient Memories

THE CHILD WATCHED in amazement. The teacher, tall, handsome, and kindly, pulled down the story from its board holder. It was like a map on which so many teachers would trace, also with a pointer. This was no map she was pointing to. It was the *Gingerbread Boy.* "See him run . . . to find his friends . . . to chase his dog." How sweet the buttons on his coat—delicious-looking raisins. "Oh, for a piece of his hand," thought the child. "The gingerbread boy wouldn't miss it." So it went for a few minutes each day.

The teacher pointed to the words roughly tracing the shapes with the pointer. The children, chorale-style, would follow the pointer and repeat after the teacher. Her voice was beautiful. She pronounced everything so clearly. Good too, for the children had so many odd accents, the young boy as well.

It was P.S. 5 in Astoria, Queens, New York City, a dark brick building surrounded by apartment houses. Atop it were set step-like ramparts in the Dutch style. This was where the reading process was begun. For this young boy, it was interesting, but not crucial. He went home or to his father's store, where he stood outside by the newspaper stand to look at the black ink that seemed to describe a variety of disasters. He took the pennies from customers who either scurried off to or debarked from the elevated trains.

Given a few minutes of quiet, he would duck into the store to slip a comic book from the rack. Some word marks, lots of interesting pictures, but no sense for a while. Then one day it happened. Three or four months into first grade and Mrs. Tillestrand's pointer demonstrations of the *Gingerbread Boy*, everything changed.

The comic book came to life, seemingly all by itself. Age of little boy? Just about 6.5 years. Even the big black ink blobs took on meaning. He remembered one of the first headlines he was able to decipher: *Hindenburg Blimp Burns.* Horrible photographs accompanied it.

How does the transformation from inchoateness to meaning take place? What is it that makes us read? Where is that pedagogical clue that can help us to stimulate normal children to read efficiently with inner satisfaction and joy?

The Reduction of Uncertainty

A child is reading silently. Oral reading slows a child and doesn't always reveal to anyone watching the more important facets of this skill. This reader's lips do not move. The eyes dart over the page, the passage finished more quickly than expected. These are the clues to the transformation.

What has happened that caused the child to slough off the mediated reading skills sometimes so arduously acquired? The child has learned something new.

This is any easy assumption. Learning something new, demonstrating an observable skill that can also be seen as the acquisition of a new internal capability is more difficult. Frank Smith (1982, pp. 9-24, 195-196) describes the process of learning to read as the reduction of uncertainty, as the child predicts his way through the written marks to find meaning. Reduction of uncertainty denotes the resolving of questions of letter and word order in which the visual marks are transformed into meaning at a rate that defies all explanations of reading as decoding to sound.

The test of this reduction of uncertainty lies in finding the meaning of the passage. The teacher asks the child questions about the passage as he/she silently completes the paragraph, page, or story. The reduction of uncertainty points to the fact that the child must already have a sense of the passage's meaning while moving along visually and mentally. The marks become the clues that help the child say "yes" or "no" to the relationships engendered in the vast array of possible letters and words that could appear.

Assuredly, the concept of "orthographic redundancy" helps to reduce the uncertainty. Certain letters come together often and predictably in common words. Other letter combinations in English are rare. Consonants "x," "c," and "q" usually are associated with certain vowels; even the raw shapes of letters give us certain expectations after awhile. More redundancy in reading occurs through an acquaintance with sentence structure—how verbs, nouns, and articles are put together in traditional sentences. Such "syntactic" redundancy also helps bring about a measure of predictability. For example, certain sentences make sense in terms of parts of speech and their function: "Girls dance with excitement and grace." Others do not: "Girls with excitement and grace dance." The child picks up, together with a sense of meaning, a wide variety of clues that lowers the uncertainty. The child also uses various pieces of overlapping information (redundancy)—spelling, grammar, letter shapes, meaning—that allow for quicker reading than speaking of material.

Yet it is not at all clear what the child is seeing as his/her eyes move rapidly across the page, even whether he/she is utilizing much logical clueing. The actual mechanism for moving beyond the mediated stage requires additional explanation. Frank Smith in attempting an explanation has demonstrated how this could not, as some have claimed, be some version of the template process in which machines can decode (read?) standardized computer-drawn numbers.

As we know, the human eye/mind can recognize a wide variety of versions of letters—"a," "A,"—that would confuse a machine. (In 1984, a computer was invented that could supposedly recognize just such variations in the shapes of the letters.) In fact, it is probable, given the rate at which even a young fluent reader reads, that he/she is not examining each letter as a whole. This young reader will "predict" the way through the text, efficiently reducing uncertainty and making a sequence of meaning guesses.

Sir James Pitman, as we noted in the previous chapter, designed the letters for I.T.A. so that their upper parts are similar to traditional orthography. Young I.T.A. scholars seem to have little difficulty in transferring their fluent reading in I.T.A. to T.O. without losing this fluency. The clue then is that children scan the upper parts of letters to gather as much visual information as possible about the shapes of the letters, combining this with other redundant information, such as syntax, or semantics, to make a series of accurate guesses as to meaning.

This process of letter, word, sentence identification is called the *feature analytic* process of learning to read. It denotes that the child "abstracts" certain features of the written material in order to glean the meaning of a word or sentence. Certainly the mind is actively at work relating the passage to other, previously gathered, knowledge so that the features (shapes) of letters and words become the clues that identify specifically and accurately the meaning of the passage.

Kenneth Goodman did the reading profession a service when he called to our attention the occurrence of miscues by all readers, mentioned earlier. Here a child accurately reads a passage, but on occasion slips in a word that may be different from that which appears on the page, but is often synonymous in meaning and appropriate syntactically, e.g., "Tim ran after the *horse*," instead of *"dog."* Not "Tim ran after the *going*," instead of *"dog."* The child has naturally not attended to the actual configuration of the words, but has allowed his/her mind to substitute for what he/she may have been too lazy to scrutinize visually.

Miscues constitute reading errors that can be important. However, in this case, they are not fatal, since the child is reading in the spirit of things, which allows him/her to move along in reducing the uncertainty, using a minimum of visual marks. The child in this case went a bit too fast and must be instructed to slow up a little, to look quickly at the entire sentence.

We see the mind at work in the "cloze procedure." Here, children are tested for comprehension and syntactic understanding by being asked to fill in letter and word blanks in various places in the sentence. Since reading is the penetration beyond the purely visual mark to the semantic message encoded in the writing, this concern for rapid reading and comprehension rather than letter, word, sound calling is wise pedagogy, even if many established authorities still affirm that reading is after all decoding the marks to their sound (natural language) equivalents, then comparing the meanings within the structure of spoken linguistic communication. Even famous professors can be mistaken about the obvious.

Mysterious Ease

It is clear that at the point of transition from mediated reading to the first stages of fluent reading—the magic moment—the child moves past the need to decode all words to sound. Certainly he/she may slow down momentarily at a new and difficult word and then use phonics techniques to work out the sound of the word. *Good* reading however, is simply too rapid for subvocalization (slight tremors of the lips as the child silently sounds out letters and words).

At the same time, are we entitled to say that our new understanding of the reading process reinstates the "look-say" method of whole-word recognition? The answer is "no," and for various reasons. Here, speed again becomes a factor. For, the child does not seem to gulp words one at a time. From a variety of experiments, it is clear that a child can find meaning when there are letter gaps in the words or even in the sequence of words. Just as the pronunciation of words is often determined by the completion of the sentence in reading, so, too, individual word meaning is determined by the place of the word in the sentence and the particular semantic or syntactic role it occupies:

> "You should *read* the book I *read* yesterday."; "Please *permit* me to get my *permit*."; "You can *bank* on the *bank* by the river *bank*." (Smith, 1971, p. 146)

If it is true that at advanced levels of fluent reading, the good reader can whiz over a page at 300 to 500 words a minute, no one today could argue that this process can accommodate a whole-word recognition theory. Even the seven- or eight-year-old child, reading quite a bit slower, is still "reducing uncertainty," reading for meaning at a rate that already makes "look-say" alone suspect as an explanation.

Features

We get closer to understanding what the "feature analytic" skills entail when we consider the classic "specific dyslectic," i.e., reading-disabled, child. While we explore this issue in greater detail later on, it is enough to note here that these children are usually neither intellectually nor semantically impaired. In other kinds of testing situations, it becomes clear that while the reading system (integrational level) is disabled, "deep-structure" intellectual function continues to operate at a high level.

We can conclude that somewhere in the processing of the incoming perceptual-visual information, there is a neurological short circuit on the way to deep-structure cognition. The child is unable to use certain redundant skills of reading (word and letter order, syntactic clues) to predict the way through the material. While there is a proliferation of sometimes subtle disabilities associated with the general class of language processing problems, the global visual-perceptual system seems to be indicted.

The stability of letter, word, and sentence order must be maintained as the child scans the page. Further, a not-yet-understood process of abstraction seems to take place as the normal child moves through the written materials. The knowledge of the relation of letters learned earlier in mediated reading (their sounds, too) to lexical units of meaning, seems to assist the youngsters in abstracting bits and pieces of these words and sentences to predict the meaning of the reading material.

A good reader needs to abstract fewer and fewer visual elements of these written materials in order to make a guess or prediction as to their meaning. We call these units of visual material "features," because they are not whole letters, words, or sentences. Each human being has his/her own repertoire of what pieces of letters, words, sentences clue him/her in to meaning. Naturally, the more intelligent, the more knowledgeable a person is, the less the need to see all the parts (features) of words and sentences.

It is this ability to absorb minute visual clues—an ascender in an "i," the rounded curves in "m" and "n," a circle or half circle in an "o" or a "c," distinctions that start the process of visual abstraction (feature analysis)—that sends the child quickly into the predictive semantic mode of rapid reading. As the reader's speed and accuracy improve, this process of visual-mental abstraction becomes more efficient—note the stories of such legendary characters as Teddy Roosevelt reading through whole pages of materials at a glance.

How It Happens

The magic moment, then, is composed of two elements. One involves the deep-structured intellectual growth of the child which underlies the semantic aspect of reading. What is the child predicting while reading rapidly over and through the symbolic markings on the page? Obviously, the intellectual expectation as to "what comes next?" determines the kinds of subliminal guesses a child is making as to letter and word features.

The second element derives from the integrational level of thought, as applied to the visual-linguistic marks on a page. Here we have a different kind of vision organized and stabilized for our minds. Those Kohler lenses spoken about earlier could not reverse the upside down field of vision for language symbols as they could objects of our perceptual world, which leads us to believe that "seeing" objects is different from "seeing" written language. Here too evidence accumulates that language perception works off a different aspect of the neurological system than our more general preceptual abilities. To abstract bits and pieces of words and letters in rapid motion—left to right, down-up-down (for we do not read merely across the page, but in jumps, or saccades, even diagonally down the page)—a shorthand message has to be communicated to the brain and the understanding.

Children develop the skills to do feature analysis at different ages. Some children are significantly delayed in the maturation of this system. The so-called intermodal connectivity of one sensory organ to the other—eyes, ears, touch (the distance receptors)—is so variously wired in each of us that our "pure" reading abilities in tune with our more general language skills can often be seriously interfered with. At the same time, such a handicapped child could have a larger intellectual potential than the average.

The magic moment denotes the maturation of those neurological elements required for feature analytic linguistic recognition. A similar auditory maturation probably occurs at an early age with regard to the natural (spoken) language, when the garble of sounds the youngster hears is distilled at about one to one and a half years of age into a coherent system of recognized phonemes (forty-four in our language) and their semantic substratum. So too with written language, the ability to move rapidly across the written code, pick out essential featural clues to predict the meaning that will enable us to choose further bits and pieces of the writing requires: (1) perceptual stability (vision), (2) a maturing integration-transmission neurological system leading into (3) deep structure, semantic understanding, which powers the overall intellectual processes of word, sentence, and paragraph recognition. True or fluent reading will then have begun.

FURTHER READINGS

Durkin, Dolores. (1974) "A six year study of children who learn to read in school at the age of four." *Reading Research Quarterly*. Vol. 10, 9-61.

Gates, Arthur I. (1937) "The necessary mental age for beginning reading." *Elementary School Journal*. Vol. 37, 497-508.

Goodman, K. (1969) "Analysis of oral reading miscues: Applied psycholinguistics." *Reading Research Quarterly*. Vol. 5, 1, 9-30.

Haber, R. N. and L. R. Haber. (1981) "The shape of a word can specify its meaning." *Reading Research Quarterly*. Vol. 3, 334-345.

MacGinitie, Walter H. (1969) "Evaluating readiness for learning to read: A critical review and evaluation of research." *Reading Research Quarterly*. Vol. 4, 396-410.

Morphett, Mable and Carleton Washburne. (1931) "When should children begin to read?" *Elementary School Journal*. Vol. 31, 496-503.

Neville, M. H. and A. K. Pugh. (1976) "Context in reading and listening: Variations in approach to Cloze tasks." *Reading Research Quarterly*. Vol. 12, 1, 13-31.

Smith, F. (1971, 1982) *Understanding reading*. New York: Holt, Rinehart and Winston.

8

Fluent Reading

A New Plateau

"WE MAKE THEM or break them by third grade," a wise old reading teacher muttered in frustration to her student teacher. "Correction," she added wearily. "There's still a long way for them to go. Plenty of opportunity for a shipwreck."

By third grade, the normal child has presumably matured neurologically and intellectually; all three systems for reading should be in place and operating. No longer does the child have to translate the visual markings into sound equivalents before comprehension takes place. The eye moves quickly over the written materials absorbing chunks of "shorthand information"; the "features" of this written material which are then rapidly brought together in short-term memory are finally processed to deep-structured meaning and understanding.

Still, it is a relatively slow process as compared to a Ph.D. candidate in his/her midtwenties, whizzing through abstract research materials. The seven- or eight-year-old child, even one whose reading system is operative at this age, is still untutored intellectually. Parents and educators must guide the novice reader in the trick of comprehension, even basic reading for thinking techniques, in order to move the child's hesitant fluency into confident exuberance and daring.

Needless to say, the requirements of reading education from about third grade on are quite different from those earlier on. It is the confusion, or even the ignorance, about the various stages of language and reading development that causes educators to engage in often inappropriate and counterproductive forms of teaching from the third grade on.

One of the clues to the uniqueness of the fluent reading stage lies in the well-accepted statistic about reading/intelligence scores of children. From the third grade on, children show a sharp separation in their reading skills, where earlier they were closely grouped in these skills. In other words, from third grade on, more intelligent children with reasonably operative reading skills pull away from their confreres, who may have also decent reading functions, but seemingly lesser intellectual abilities.

The reason for this is that in the younger children, five to eight years of age, the more purely readiness and reading skills (perceptual and integrational levels) dominated the picture of reading development and instruction. For obvious reasons, the intellectual dimension stayed in the background as the children learned about shapes and sounds and their interrelationships. The cognitive content of the stories, even given the immaturity of the children, was necessarily quite modest, certainly below the children's auditory understanding. Thus we could observe some children who learned their sound/sight decoding skills quite well and who even moved easily into the early stages of "feature identification" fluent reading, gradually, in the middle grades, begin to falter in their reading progress.

The danger for parents and teachers here lies in the possible misidentification of children who have difficulty getting into the fluent reading stage. These are the children who suffer from reading system short circuits (integrational level). They typically can see and hear, they appear to be alert and bright, pick things up quickly, they react to the world around them with sensitivity and receptivity. Yet their reading and writing suffer from all kinds of consternating impediments. A close analysis of their learning plight will often reveal not a failure of deep-structure "predicting one's way through the visual print," rather, a wide variety of specific reading and writing, sometimes even listening and speaking, disabilities. Here, the educational solution takes on quite a different prognosis. Calling for the help of specialists and their technical expertise and equipment is highly recommended. Often a probable diagnosis of dyslexia will present itself.

Sometimes children who just have not been exposed to careful, steady, systematic reading instruction are cavalierly diagnosed as dyslectic. The solution for such an inadequately-prepared child is usually less television, more family reading, discussion, cultural stimulation, as well as intensive, systematic classroom reading instruction. We must remember that in this stage of a child's fluent reading, merely continuing the decoding tradition of mediated reading will do little for long-term language growth.

Decoding is a necessary crutch at a certain stage in the child's development. From that point on, it can be used to sound out new and more complicated words. Sometimes sounding out a word will trigger recognition. Even at the intermediate grade level, it is not crucial that a child sound out all new words. We often chuckle at children's mispronunciation of complicated words that they may have read but never heard pronounced. This occurs often with precocious children, or even adult unschooled readers. Yet, it is crucial to the sounding out of a word for one to have heard a word in order to recognize it. A wise teacher encourages children to read difficult material even at the price of their mispronouncing some new words.

What is most important is that the child confront and guess at new words in context. Mispronunciation is remediable through schooling. By contrast, inability to understand new words in reasonable paragraph context is often a sign of poor comprehension and weak intelligence.

We can conclude these observations on the attainment of fluent reading with the emphasis on the need for a new phase of reading instruction. Here, steady day-by-day, week-by-week sessions with the teacher ought to emphasize the varying intellectual and content skills whereby the child increasingly utilizes less visual information and more redundant syntactic and semantic knowledge. It is not enough to hear and see things that will stretch the mind. The child now needs to read enormous quantities of different kinds of materials and to learn to think linguistically, through words, sentences, and paragraphs. The key question is whether the child is predicting the way through the material with understanding. Here an intelligent teacher excels at challenging the child with ever new but appropriate reading, thinking, and writing tasks, tasks that excite and stimulate.

Approaches to Understanding

Most teachers today are aware that mouthing the words on a primer's page is not reading. Thus the test of reading competency is not necessarily the ability to read orally. The teacher does not have to hear the child read in order to state that a stage of reading fluency has been accomplished.

Silent reading by the child, where comprehension is confirmed by careful questioning after the passage has been completed, is often quite enough. The element of sound has thus been eliminated as an important aspect of reading. What about a child who while reading silently moves a finger along the page, often with the eyes following? Sometimes we even find a child who has not completely surmounted the mediated reading stage, moving a finger over the letters and words, but now in the roughly up and down configuration following the shapes of the letters and words. If a child does the latter, it is virtually impossible for him/her to overcome short-term memory (S.T.M.) blockages to reading comprehension.

Our challenge in this latter case, as in all other instances of children who need to surmount the various crutches of mediated reading—slow visual processing, tedious phonic decoding, use of fingers and other propriocentric devices—is to find ways of getting large enough chunks of reading materials into the short- and long-term memory systems for comprehension to take place. Once this occurs and the "magic slate" of S.T.M. is cleared for new information, we can at last approach a process of fluent reading for meaning. Only then can we avoid the often agonizing gulping of small bits of reading materials in which the mistaught child engages.

A number of years ago, Jospeh Wepman, of the University of Chicago, proposed what he called the "modality concept." He here called for teachers not to anchor their approaches to children's learning to read on only one method. Every child, having his/her own particular neurological organization, inevitably has a particular learning bias. The key requirement is that a child be able through sight, sound, touch, head, body, or hand movements, to process the visual symbols in such a way that they be translated into useful grammatical structures for comprehension.

Teach the child to his/her strength was his dictum. Once the child finds his/her own best way of "encoding the visual marks to meaning," often the "crutches" that were utilized to make the transition will be abandoned. The child, having gained a technique of accessing long-term memory, will need less and less purely preceptual or physical information. Since we read with our intellect, once we have "gotten the idea," we search for our most efficient procedure.

Since reading is a matter of mind over matter, the route to fluent reading is not nearly as important as the attainment of the goal. When that is achieved, the whole ballgame changes. Even moderately handicapped children with a clear-cut reading disability, once having gotten the idea of extracting meaning from the symbols, can flourish in other educational areas, even if their language skills are not the most highly developed.

This brings up another interesting fact about the inter-correlation of the symbolic systems of learning of which fluent reading is one of the important handmaidens. The Johns Hopkins University study of mathematically precocious youth (SMPY) has dredged up some interesting facts. The children in question are usually junior-high-school-aged, eleven to fourteen. Quite a few twelve-year-olds among the group achieved 800 S.A.T. scores in the math section usually given to seventeen- and eighteen-year olds. While much is made today about the supposedly independent character of such symbol skills, virtually all of these youngsters received extremely high verbal scores on their S.A.T.'s, although not in the spectacular range of their mathematics scores.

An explanation is easy. We are here witnessing the process of intelligent thought expressing itself through diverse intellectual modalities. It stands to reason that a child who has unlocked the secret of meaningful thinking and is free of any significantly disabling learning problems could show the power of his/her intelligence in a variety of symbolic expressions. Remember, for children in kindergarten, the most predictive of the reading readiness tests for future reading success is the number concepts subtest.

Assisting Fluency—A

The overriding idea of this chapter has been to emphasize that the process of reading competency is attained only if we carefully bear in mind what reading is from the middle grades on. Basically, the reading process now is skill building in the areas in which the mind becomes competent in careful, systematic discursive or logical thought. Reading, as we have shown, started out in history first as an aid to memory, a way to order the environment, help in trade, commerce, industry, in all those matters that are crucial to a highly developed urban civilization.

Certain kinds of thinking flourish in the ordinary give and take of social life, without reading or school learning. Certainly intelligence does not exhaust its potentialities in bookishness. Too often, however, we are deceived as we observe active, seemingly bright, quick young readers. Some of these, when we analyze their reading closely, find academic learning quite difficult in any of the symbolic abstract areas. Too often we forget that this kind of learning—reading, arithmetic, musical notation—is a special skill. It does not come by itself.

Our minds need to be trained to work through reading materials. This requires practice, discipline, and the kind of schooling that will guide the child through the particular logical subject matter workout. The key is the steady day-by-day process of instruction that will expose the child to a variety of challenges and thus expand horizons and fluency with the thinking demands of the written word. Educational negligence in this area is the prime cause of the virtually functional illiteracy of so many junior high school students. They have not been exposed to and required to do the hard but gratifying work of reading for meaning.

Quickly we must add that reading is more than a discipline in the intellectual sphere. It is also for the growth of the soul, the esthetic and moral dimensions. A reading program must also include fun and enrichment elements. Too often, the basal readers constitute the entirety of the reading program; social studies and science texts are used for fact learning, losing for the child another crucial element for language and thinking development.

Thus it is clear that the essence of improvement and advance through the fluent reading stage lies in the development of the child's various mental powers, appreciation of esthetic, literary element in reading, the power of logical thought, even problem solving. The growth of all of these skills will ultimately lead the individual toward the higher professions and responsibilities of civilized life.

Assisting Fluency—B

Now to some of the tricks of the trade. Many children learn these naturally as part of their eager immersion in reading. Others, for no special reason, don't fall into these things spontaneously; they need a bit of help.

Inadequate speed in moving across a page of written material is one of the commonest deficiencies of inexperienced and timid readers. Part of the problem of inadequate speed in the eye movements is caused by malinstruction at the mediated reading level where teachers insist on letter/sound identification. This breaks up the reading flow and doubly confuses readers, because the latter internally perceive the irrelevancy of what they are doing, often blaming themselves for not understanding the rationale of decoding and thus further inhibiting their spontaneity.

The great problem in this form of reading "constipation" is of course the blockage in short-term memory that such reading produces. Children must be taught to move their eyes rapidly across the page so that they can gather big enough chunks of visual material to allow the passing of this material through short-term to long-term memory.

For the lazy, frustrated, or timid eye, there is that old standby, the moving finger. In the old days, teachers would have been aghast at such a solution, but here, the ends should determine the means. Once the child discovers the thrill of reading rapidly, now for meaning, and without frustrating comprehension problems caused by "tunnel vision," the finger will soon be relegated to scratching the ear or tapping the desk. The eye will take off now at the beckon of the mind. No finger will be able to keep up.

As Joseph Wepman would argue: do not remediate the wounded learning modality, exploit the usable means of learning, for it will transform the child. Crutches of learning—eye, ear, finger—will wither away as important means, once the mind understands that it is in control of the reading systems. Here the end really does determine the means.

In other cases, children have difficulty focusing on a line of print, partially because they are not able to put into effect the smooth rhythmic left-to-right visual motion. No law prohibits a parent or teacher from putting an opaque piece of paper under the line to be read and then systematically increasing the speed at which each line is revealed by lowering the masking piece of paper. Of course these are only early procedures that may facilitate an increase in speed where difficulties occur during the fluent reading stage.

For older readers, such as college students, who are having difficulty with their pace of reading, the simple crutches that we create for younger children will not do. Commercial reading programs such as the Evelyn Wood approach have accumulated some empirical evidence as to how to help people to read faster, for better comprehension, without the theoretical elegance provided by psycholinguistics.

Several concepts arise from an analysis of how we read that will help us understand the *why* behind the practical suggestions: (a) "Saccade": this is the jump that the eye makes while moving over the page. We do not merely stare at reading material. The eye must move. The key element is that these saccades move over the page systematically and efficiently. When the eye lands again, a "fixation" will occur.

(b) A "fixation" avails the eye and mind of an opportunity to gulp information from the page. All adults in reading make between three and four fixations per second. An inexperienced reader will make a shade fewer fixations and will probably absorb less information at each landing. The natural pathway of the experienced fluent reader is diagonally down the page (left to right). This is why using the opaque paper (as outlined above) has to be only a temporary stage in the speeding-up of the reading process.

Saccades and fixations are only part of the story. The eye goes back, seemingly to check on itself, perhaps to confirm and fill out what it thought it saw. (c) This is called a "regression." Too many regressions and we will know that our information absorption during the fixations down the page was inefficient. Perhaps the saccades themselves were not rhythmic or coherent.

Note that here too the mind's eye must take in enough information in its fixations so that comprehension can occur with a minimum number of confirming regressions. They say that Teddy Roosevelt trained himself in this way intuitively; he was able to read a page at one quick glance. This merely means that he got an overall idea of the content of relatively simple material. Complex reading that needs careful thought will not accept such once-over-lightly rates of speed.

It is not too far-fetched to compare the mind in the reading process to a radar complex. The eye is the antenna, directed by a complex series of electrical controls (integrational system), themselves under the logical discipline of a plan (semantic/deep-structure, long-term memory) that seeks out the blips of information that hit the antenna. Conceive of these antennae as the eye, the moving controls and translation of

116

the electrical blips on the antennae surfaces to recognizable images of planes, birds, "things" (the integrational system). However the operation and planning of the whole are guided by the mind (semantic/deep-structure), which directs the movement of the antennae and interprets the electronics into tangible concepts.

Peripheral vision becomes crucial here, because looking at words is not enough. Words are embedded in sentences and paragraphs and derive their meaning from the larger whole. This movement of the eyes diagonally down the page and up again often has to be learned as part of the process of achieving reading efficiency. The child must also learn how to adjust speeds of eye and mind movements to the relative difficulty of the material. Not only is comprehension at stake here, but also enjoyment. The issue of proper rates of speed for easiest comprehension in fluent reading thus applies to fiction as well as nonfiction.

A final note on the improvement of fluent reading efficiency is directed at overall comprehension strategy, especially for the student in the junior or senior high school and college levels. When approaching new study materials, most students plunge in and engage in a titanic paragraph-by-paragraph onslaught against new reading matter. Witness any number of used textbooks. The underlinings are awesome. We can almost perceive the sentence-by-sentence regimen as the students read through "the new stuff."

Careful study is, of course, always necessary. However, some approaches are more efficient than others. One suggestion might be to read the assigned material as quickly as possible just to gain a general idea of the content and the author's direction (logical/pedagogical). The reader will be amazed at how much awareness and understanding can be picked up even in such a quick reading.

The "radar system" mind seeks to find the meaning in this material, for few things we read are completely foreign to us. We pick up much more than we think, especially if we are not paralyzed (as in tunnel vision) into seeing only the two or three words directly before our eyes. Then, when we return to reading the material more carefully, we already know the ending (which helps) and the author's direction. Now we have context and thus can judge the relative importance of what we are reading for the purpose of underlining. We will therefore do this less, and hit only the most important material.

Probably the total time that we spend on a given assigned amount of reading matter will turn out to be the same or less. However, the level of comprehension is bound to be higher than in the frustrating line-by-line analysis in which so many students engage. It is impossible not to believe that a great deal of S.T.M. breakdown, short-circuiting comprehension, arises from this kind of tedious word by word study.

Conclusion

The process of creating meaning out of print is given a tremendous boost when the child matures neurologically to the point of being able to abstract letters, words, even sentences from bits and pieces of the written material. Certainly intelligence is involved in making these guesses and subsequent confirmations. More important is a series of unknown internal assists from the perceptual/nervous system that translates the messages, routes them in space and time, and sorts them into a structure of meanings.

Some very intelligent children suffer from one or more of a variety of malfunctions of this system in which the featural shorthand integration of marks into meaning doesn't happen. For those many who search for a different modality for learning, reading now turns into a special and difficult challenge to their schooling and their intelligence.

For what we have in written material are ideas, special kinds of ideas that tell us things more efficiently than if we only looked at the outside world, or simply talked and listened to people. It is obviously easier to learn new things out on the street or in the playground, even watching the T.V. at home. Learning to read and write is difficult and tedious and in the beginning it is sometimes simplistic. However, these are skills that much later in life will yield knowledge far beyond the street or the home. The knowledge gained through reading and writing will lead to the mastery of other kinds of symbolic skills—in the world of mathematics and the sciences, in computer logic, in musical notation and composition—that in turn will open up vast new realms of human knowledge and power.

The written language is the beginning of the pathway that reveals the power of the human mind, thought, and intelligence. Fluent reading is where it all begins. Further, human language is a marvelous facilitator for human thought. In many ways it has developed in tandem with the growth of the human brain. One can see language, both by ear (the natural spoken language) and by eye (the invented written forms) as part of this midrange integrational neurological system.

Thus reading and writing are means toward the goal of empowering our intelligence with new and significant tools. We must teach children in the beginning stages and even on further to see their language as a crucial tool for learning. Other forms of learning cannot be substituted for reading and writing. Practice, skill building, and almost complete immersion are necessary for one to learn how to think and act through the written medium.

The achieved fluency derives from the mind's ability to work through the visual marks at speeds that go beyond mere looking. In predicting our way through written material, our minds are beginning to work and model in a new and portentous clay. As long as we think along these lines, using language as a tool, we will not neglect the kinds of systematic disciplined learning that are necessary to reveal the many layers of knowledge that lie latent in this miraculous medium.

FURTHER READINGS

Abromovici, S. (1984) "Lexical information in reading and memory." *Reading Research Quarterly*. Winter, 173-187.

Berger, A. (1970) *Speed Reading*. Newark, Del.: International Reading Association.

Clark, M. (1976) *Young fluent readers*. London: Heinemann.

Duffy, G. G. et al, eds. (1984) *Comprehension instruction: Perspectives and suggestions*. New York: Longman.

Durkin, D. (1978-1979) "What classroom observations reveal about reading comprehension instruction." *Reading Research Quarterly*. Vol. 14, 481-533.

Flood, J. ed. (1984) *Understanding reading comprehension: Cognition, language, and the structure of prose*. Newark, Del.: International Reading Association.

Pearson, P. D. and M. C. Gallagher. (1983) "The instruction of reading comprehension." *Contemporary Educational Psychology*. Vol. 8, 317-344.

Stanley, J. C. et al., eds. (1977) *The gifted and the creative: A fifty year perspective*. Baltimore: Johns Hopkins.

Wepman, J. M. (1964) "The perceptual basis for learning," in *Reading and the language arts*. Chicago: University of Chicago Press, pp. 25-33.

9

The Phonics Fallacy

Politics

Y OU MAY WELL ask how reading instruction ever got
mixed up in politics. That it did is no myth. Groups like
the *Council for Basic Education,* well-meaning in and of
themselves—advocating one reading method over another,
attacking the political complexion of an educational profession once inextricably involved in look-say reading pedagogy—inevitably set the tone of the post-World War II decades
debate.

This is the first argument against phonics, a caution to
all parents and teachers to beware crusading for a panacea
that owes its programmatic momentum more to political action than to educational efficacy. It can fairly be said that for
all the uneven results of look-say, its original stimulus was
scientific; it was an earnest attempt to introduce modern

ideas into the profession. That the public school establishment itself became highly politicized in the first half of the twentieth century is beside the point. The two issues, reading instruction and the social and political tilt of the educational leadership, are entirely separate.

One can understand the frustration of thoughtful people from all sectors of the political spectrum to see their educational expectations for universal high literacy dissolve before their eyes. The search for the villains in the drama was, sadly, an inevitability. As we shall point out in the final chapter, however, there are deeper causes for our educational decline, including reading, than a mere methodology, even if flawed. By the mid-1980's, it is clear that the overthrow of the progressivist tradition in education, the supplementation of look-say with heavy doses of phonics instruction has hardly moved reading effectiveness forward. In fact, a generation of young people is coming to maturity whose reading problems are as severe as at any time in the past, only today the contemporary etiology wags its fingers at over-zealous phonics instruction.

This is a plea to remove reading from the realm of a political/religious crusade. We need instead to turn it back onto the high road of dispassionate factual analysis based on sound scientific theoretical principles.

Efficiency

The by now classic study of the efficiency of phonics analysis was completed in 1969 by Berdiansky et al. It analyzed 9000 words that six- to nine-year-olds normally encounter as part of their education. Of these words, one-third were more than two syllables and thus rather complex for the truly beginning reader. The other 6000 words were studied to

see how a phonics analysis could be used to develop pedagogical rules to help guide the young reader through the reading process, eventually to decode new words to sound, then
to meaning.

It was found that these 6000 one-syllable words involved
166 rules, sixty involving the pronunciation of consonants
and 106 involving single or complex vowels. In addition,
forty-five sound-to-letter correspondences were unique and
thus involved no rule, at least in those 6000 words. The reader must bear in mind that these were simple words, words
that youngsters in the primary grades would encounter.

As Frank Smith, who first provided a summary of this
evidence, states,

> There is the possibility that reliance on phonics will involve
> readers in so much delay that short-term memory will be
> overloaded, and they will lose the sense of what they are
> reading. A tendency to rely exclusively on phonic rules may
> create a handicap for beginning readers whose biggest prob-
> lem is [the need] to develop speed in reading. Our working
> memories do not have an infinite capacity and reading [com-
> prehension] is not a task that can be accomplished at too lei-
> surely a pace. (Smith, 1982, p. 141)

One of the great difficulties in using phonics to find
meaning in reading material is that even in a short word, one
must usually read the end of the word before one knows how
to pronounce the beginning. Thus, a beginning reader, using
phonics rules, moving slowly from left to right, has to return
right to left for many words, e.g., "father," "fathead," "telephone," "shepherd." Better to know the word in advance or
learn to sweep through the visual material in an unpedantic
left-to-right sequence.

The "o" in "non," "howl," "whole," "sow," "holly,"
"cool," or "down" simply evades any specific rule that could
assist pronunciation. Much better to know the words from
the spoken language, both meaning and pronunciation, and

read exclusively for meaning; the proper sounding-out will come along at its own pace.

Even a well-developed oral vocabulary is no sure guide to reading for meaning. For example, Carol Chomsky shows how useful nonphonetical spelling and pronunciations are in helping us to see the relationships within a group of familiar words. Were we to use I.T.A. or any other phonics approach, we might lose our awareness of their "lexical" or meaning relationships: The words "bomb," "bombardier," "bombing," "bombardment" or "sign" and "signature" *sound* unrelated. Yet the written words, even in this odd relationship of print to sound, announce their meaning (lexical) relationship with each other. Reliance on the phonics or sounding-out approach would give us little appreciation of the peculiar pattern.

What often happens in a classroom in which reading is taught through phonics rules is that the teacher follows a line of least resistance. Only the most obvious and common vowel and consonant sounds are taught. This would include variable vowel pronunciations and consonants in combination that alter pronunciation. Beyond that they hope for the best with all the rest of the so-called phonics rules. What this means is that there is already a tacit acknowledgment that the rules as taught in the first two or three grades will suffice to facilitate meaning by decoding to the sound of the natural language. The expectation is that fluent reading will occur automatically as a by-product of teaching these few simple but inclusive rules.

No parent or teacher would long want to hear the children reading orally as if they were sounding out words: "Ch/il-dr/en are pl/ay/ing w/i/th my ba/by bro/th/er." The question that we must ask the phonics advocates is this: "If you don't want a reader to continue to read in this halting phonics decoding manner, then please explain how the child will make the transfer from sounding out words to fluent, rapid reading for meaning." The phonics partisan has no answer from within his theory except to argue that a transition will take place *somehow*. Today, few still claim that good readers continue decoding to sound. As recently as 1974, Charles Walcutt would write as follows in his influential textbook *Teaching Reading:*

> Reading awareness means mastering the code by which spoken words are represented in visual, spatial symbols. . . . Obviously, to be really aware of what he is doing the child must be aware of what writing is and what reading it involves: turning printed symbols into sounds and knowing that those sounds are words that carry meanings. He must also inevitably learn how our writing, imperfect as it is, nevertheless is a system for symbolizing the sounds of language on the printed page. (p. 245)

Thus the urgency for phonics instruction derives from a theory about the relationship of the written form of language to the spoken form. Phonics advocates from the phonic linguistic school believe that the written form is derivative in a conceptual sense, that in order to understand what is written (reading) we must first have decoded the written material to its sound equivalent.

As we noted in chapter 4, all of this has been resoundingly refuted. True, written language came into being long after spoken language had been in use (by at least a million or so years). Yet it does not follow that, to be understood, all writing must be first correlated with speech. For a myriad number of factual reasons this is not true, and those who believe that it is true and base their reading theories on such assumptions put the novice reader through a pedagogical meat grinder.

To demonstrate that the above statement is not mere hyperbole, I challenge the reader to decipher Professor Walcutt's description as to how the child attains to reading meaning through the use of what he calls systematic phonics-decoding teaching:

He will be working with increasing ease and success on his decoding skill, which increasingly builds up a store of proper "recognition" words, a storehouse of images that he recognizes instantly. As the decoding skill becomes more and more an automatic behavioral response, he will no longer have to "close his eyes and listen to himself" when he learns a new word; now he will respond to it in terms of clusters of letters, which are already firm sound-images in his brain. By the second or third grade, the child, when seeing for the first time a word that he knows by ear, will say it right off—or even hear it in his mind's ear without verbalizing it. When the child comes to an unfamiliar word, he will say it more or less correctly, and then know how to learn what it means. (p. 246)

What Professor Walcutt seems to be saying in this passage is that while the child is decoding input visual images to sound, comprehension of a word will *somehow* take place. It is, however, more an act of faith than an experimentally predictable or rational explanation as to how the transfer from sound to meaning can take place in the rapid tempo required for fluent reading.

Phonics advocates thus have no answer, no scientifically supportable explanation, as to why they are using phonics in the first place. Most teachers, being rational, practical people, don't impose on their students that full panoply of phonics rules and exceptions for both oral reading and spelling. After a few inductive generalizations, students usually have to wing it much as did the "look-sayers." In addition, the slow letter-by-letter and syllable-by-syllable approach cannot possibly help a child achieve a normal reading pace, even when the reading material is as simple as the hometown newspaper. Despite the universal recognition of the need to read and comprehend rapidly, none among the phonics advocates recognizes this disjunction between the substance, methodology, and ultimate results of phonics teaching and the substance and results of good reading, as universally acknowledged by pedagogues.

Heritage

Just as the look-say method, on the basis of good practical evidence, by itself failed to lift generations into the reading stratosphere, so too a generation of phonics instruction has reaped its own peculiar educational heritage. What happens to a child when the reading process is too severely regimented into the phonics mold is that the child turns away from the naturalness of his/her purely linguistic modality and begins to analyze intellectually the phonics probabilities of, for instance, letter clusters. The slow, gnarled sounding-out of words not only blockades the normal development of featural analysis of language materials simply because of the mental effort required, but also subjects the actual search for the meaning of words and sentences to secondary status.

The result, even after systematic or explicit phonics instruction begins to wane after third grade (how long can all the children be so tortured?), is often a crippled reader. If by some good fortune a child has learned to read fluently and rapidly, it is because he/she has carved out the mental room to fly off in another direction. Perhaps it was a sensitive teacher, even with luck, a negligent one, who freed the child. The normal synthesizing work of the perceptual system in reducing to a featural shorthand the letters and words that make up reading matter and the process of comprehension will here have spontaneously come into action.

In phonics teaching, comprehension is presumed to take place *after* written matter is decoded to sound and recognized from pronunciation (even subvocally as in the half-silent reader). To the phonics advocate, the immediate comprehension of visual features, as the mind rapidly looks for confirmation or disconfirmation of educated semantic guesses, is part of an unknown world in reading.

What happens in phonics teaching is that the natural visual linguistic (integrational) system is ignored as an aid in

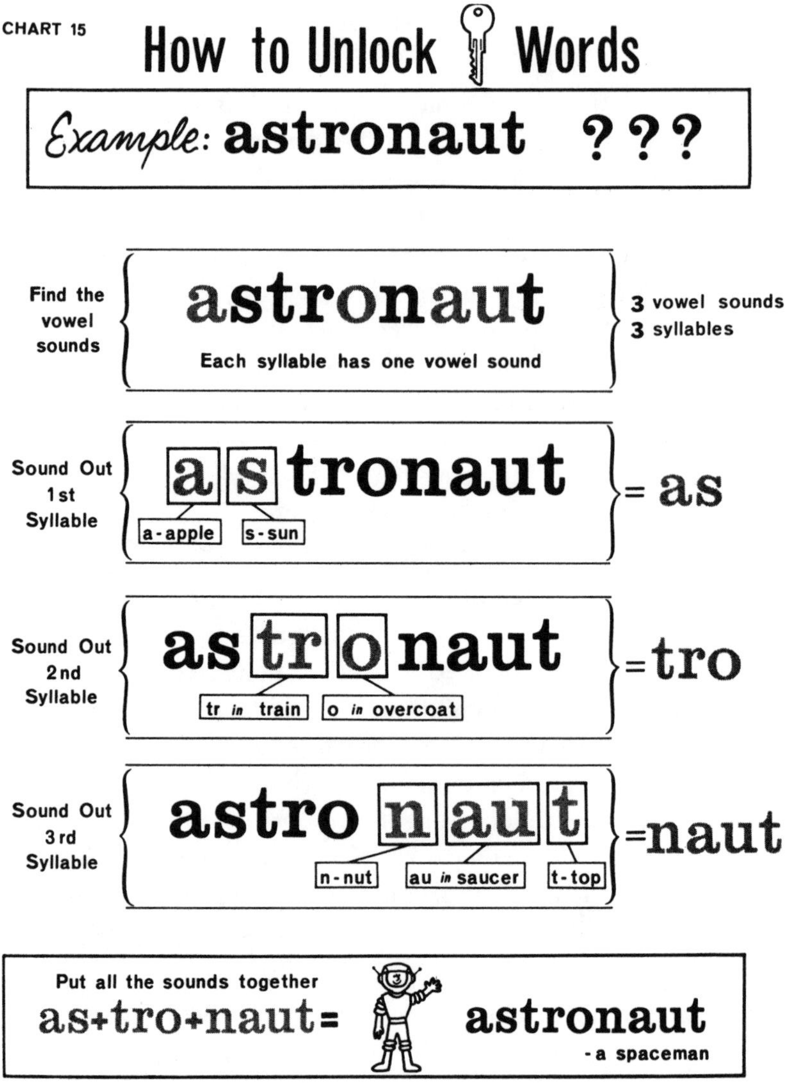

CHART 15

How to Unlock 🔑 Words

Example: **astronaut ???**

Find the vowel sounds — **astronaut**
Each syllable has one vowel sound
— **3** vowel sounds
3 syllables

Sound Out 1st Syllable — a s **tronaut**
a - apple   s - sun
= as

Sound Out 2nd Syllable — **as** tr o **naut**
tr *in* train   o *in* overcoat
= tro

Sound Out 3rd Syllable — **astro** n au t
n - nut   au *in* saucer   t - top
= naut

Put all the sounds together
as+tro+naut = 🧑‍🚀 **astronaut**
- a spaceman

Figure 5 Systematic Phonics
Systematic phonics instruction taught by rule.
(Chart 15 from Bremner Davis: *The Sound Way to Easy Reading.*)

128

reading. Instead, a wholly inefficient and self-contradictory theoretical "system" of letter-to-sound relationships saps the child's cognitive efforts. Short-term memory, as Frank Smith notes, is constantly overloaded and breakdowns in concentration and comprehension become the rule. The youngster lives in a halfway house; fear and frustration can never be transcended because a mental set now controls natural potentiality. Later on, of course, remedial and special speed-reading courses can overcome some of these bad habits.

What with the great concern for reading achievement in our time, the child, desperate to succeed, relies on the wisdom of its elders. When early on, reading is so badly taught, a method, a habit, is indelibly branded into the child's approach to all reading matter. Because of the enormous effort needed to extract meaning from the text children do not enjoy reading. This has resulted in a generation of incompetent readers. When children do have to read, even a novel, the going is slow, else the guilt is great, the results inevitable: a tragic lack of fulfillment of intellectual potential.

This does not happen to every child. As we have emphasized, many are the independent souls who escape the net of systematic phonics training and the consequent emasculation of their reading potential. More often than not, the result is *not* the production of a nonreader, as often happens with over-reliance on the visual system and whole-word identification in the look-say method. Rather, with phonics, probably a greater percentage of children become "readers." Here, however, the overall toll is more devastating because most of the normal children who learn to read through look-say (integrational system) develop into good, fluent readers. Perhaps some become weak spellers and sounders-out of new and difficult words. However, they are not lacking in word identification or general comprehension. We now have the evidence of a generation of phonics instruction, a sad, if not wholly unexpected, result.

Inductive Phonics

This chapter is not a diatribe against phonics. It is a rejection of dogmatism and ideology. As we noted in the sixth chapter, there is indeed a role for phonics analysis. It is an important stage in the progression toward rapid as well as deep understanding in reading. The phase of reading that we have called mediated reading, a stage that should vary in duration with each child, encompasses the use of phonics.

The real question ought to involve our overall educational attitude toward phonics and how we apply it in the reading program. Between the preparatory stage (reading readiness) and the transition to fluent reading, most children need to learn the basic design of our alphabetic system and how it mirrors, however, imperfectly, the phonemic structure of the spoken idiom. How much does the child need to be clued in, how much actual instruction in the correlation of such grapheme sound units ought we undertake?

Here no rule will apply equally to every child. Obviously, children whose visual-perceptual integration systems are well-wired will need only the fewest of phonetic clues to learn that those marks called letters or words mean something in the same way as do the blurry sounds of our spoken language. Then through the use of redundancy, understanding the spoken language, syntactic and semantic clues, they will begin to distill the marks of such letters and words into feature lists, a visual shorthand for the meaning that lies beneath the surface markings. In no time, they will be predicting their way through reading material, visual, integration, and semantic systems working in harmony.

Teachers will need to take another tack with children who find it harder to make the phonetic correlations between the spoken medium and the written material. For these children, the instruction ought to be devoid of heavy burdens of rule learning. The teaching of phonics ought to be by concrete example. Let the children make the inductive leaps. Do not impose the double handicap on their cognitive faculty of having simultaneously to penetrate the meaning of a word or sentence, catapulting beyond the time blockade of short-term memory, and recalling the particular phonics rules that are invoked by various grapheme units.

Mediated reading ought to be taught as a form of inductive or implicit phonics for the less visually oriented child. This child would need more auditory help in moving over the written material. Perhaps the featural distillations of fluent reading will here come slower and later for seven- or eight-year-olds. These youngsters may need more practice in working through and recalling the various shapes of letters and words before they become familiar. Phonics teaching at this stage ought to be thought of as a temporary crutch. Gradually, the child will move beyond the rehearsals of sound and plunge directly into deep-structure understanding.

Again, one cannot predict that the slow starter will not become an excellent, efficient, insightful reader. This child's integrational facility probably lies within the vast range of variation that we find in all humans. The point is that inductive (implicit) phonics be thought of by the teacher and parent as a momentary expedient on the way to more long-term skills of reading and cognition.

Self-knowledge

Here we venture a tentative, even modest hypothesis, suggested by the above material. Children aged six to ten are able to look at themselves more objectively than in the early egocentric stages of postinfancy. No deep mystic probing of the subterranean caverns of the psyche is here indicated, of course, yet the modest awareness of self, of differences between the "I" and the "thou"—and all that these distinctions connote in terms of physical comparisons, even of skills and talents—reveals that the child now lives in several worlds.

Could we mold this growing self-awareness into a greater understanding of the child's particualr learning modalities? In reading, three systems are operative: 1. the sensory-perceptual, to receive the incoming stimulus; 2. the integrational, to organize the stimulus and arrange the intermodal transformations that allow it to pass down to the 3. semantic cognition, intellectual level. Because every child has certain peculiar valences of mind—neurological organization, skills and talents—as well as different levels of deep-structured intelligence, it is virtually impossible for a teacher to learn enough about the child's submerged individuality to plan out the best reading program for each unqiue individual.

Dare we explain to the child the task at hand—the need to be able to encode the shapes, bits and pieces of letters and words to meaning? That in order to make the black marks tell us a story, we must first relate them to the language that we all speak and understand? That the first step is to learn what sounds, concretely and inductively arrived at, the letters in combination, stand for? This is so that we can get an idea of what set of marks is equivalent to each word? How best to do this? Perhaps we should give the child choices: how much phonics assistance, silent or oral reading, etc.

This suggestion may be a small step in the search for the ever evanescent grail of the perfect method of teaching reading. Yet it seems reasonable that allowing the child to enter its own arena of self-development, if proposed with care, method, and circumspection, might reveal to us new paths for confronting the dizzying variability of learning styles, talents, and modalities in the individual human being that confront modern scientific reading pedagogy today.

FURTHER READINGS

Berdiansky, Betty et al. (1969) "Spelling-sound relations . . ." *Southwest Regional Laboratory for Educational Research and Development.* Technical report #15.

Chall, J. (1983) *Learning to read: The great debate,* 2nd ed. New York: McGraw Hill.

Chomsky, C. (1970) "Reading, writing, and phonology." *Harvard Educational Review.* Vol. 40, 2, 287-309.

Hull, M. A. (1981) *Phonics for the teacher of reading,* 3rd ed. Columbus, Ohio: C. E. Merrill.

National Institute of Education. (1985) *Becoming a nation of readers.* Champaign, Ill: The Center for the Study of Reading, pp. 36-48.

Smith, F. (1982) *Understanding reading,* 3rd. ed. New York: Holt, Rinehart, Winston.

Walcutt, C. et al. (1974) *Teaching reading.* New York: Macmillan.

Williams, J. P. (1985) "The case for explicit decoding instructions", in J. Osborne et al., eds. *Reading education: Foundations for a literate America,* 205-213. Lexington, Mass: Lexington Books.

10

Disabled Readers

Introduction

IN VIEWING THE short history of worldwide literacy, we should thus not be surprised at the extent of the reading problems in as polyglot a society as the United States. Literally, the world is represented in our nation. The vast upheaval of populations, the explosion in numbers throughout the world must tell us something. The slow building up of literacy throughout the civilized world has obviously been short-circuited in our century. The decline in the character and quality of what we do and can read testifies to our extremely critical problem.

Few nations, however, are willing to face up to the larger questions of literacy and culture. Rather we see the end result of these broader demographic and social trends in the schools. The entire burden falls on the educator. While this is grossly unfair, teachers are in no position to point the finger of guilt.

The most that can be done is to describe accurately the

general nature of reading disabilities, their structure and causes. By exposing these causes to the light of reason, we might be able to assign responsibility more evenhandedly. One suspects that this will ease the teacher's task and even improve remediation. A realistic evaluation of the causes may thus produce more realistic goals.

The Three Disabilities

Just as three organic systems help to make possible the process of reading, so too there are three basic categories of disabled readers. First are those with impaired receptive function, the blind and the deaf. Even here, in what on the surface may seem to be a simple disability (given that the extent of deafness or blindness may vary), there are further complications. This is true especially in deafness, which may be accompanied by a host of other complex neurological impairments.

The second involves disabilities of the integrational system. This system exposes to us the greatest extent and complexity of reading disabilities. This is where we find specific dyslexia and with it a myriad of subtle variations on the general theme of language disabilities (general speech aphasias), often associated with perceptual and motor dysfunctions, all of which do not necessarily involve the deeper cognitive intellective functions of the individual.

Third, the category of disabilities in the intellectual system reveals a reader who, while able to perform all the basic language/perceptual requirements of reading, fails in comprehension. Whether reading haltingly with phonics assistance or struggling with featural analysis, this reader indicates a general slowing of performance that can only be explained by an intellectual deficit.

Sensory/Perceptual Disabled

Since the tactile function is the least crucial of the long-distance sensory receptors (seeing, hearing, touch) for reading we don't usually encounter such a disability in a reading setting. Rarely does an individual lose all these functions at once and still perform well enough to require instruction in reading.

Certainly the blind individual, in learning Braille, has a rough parallel spatial sense within which to learn to read. Touch reading of course lacks the eye's ability to flash saccade-like over the page, gulping increasingly larger amounts of perceptual featural clues. The Braille reader is limited to ten fingers for traversing a page of reading materials. This limits the rapidity and spontaneity of comprehension that are so much facilitated by rapid visual regressions over the page, even in reading material of relatively easy content.

The recent trend toward talking books for the blind has proven an emotionally satisfying supplement to Braille because of the human contact inherent in such a library of different books. Here different readers lend a personal element. Talking books have changed the reading "balance" for the blind. The traditional objection to the listening modality for the blind is that in listening one can lose sequential details, this compared to the quick recall of the usual visual/tactile page-turning of sight readers. With modern tape recorders, this objection is now softened. At the touch of a finger, the tape can be reversed and prior material accessed to prime the memory.

The great advantage of the blind reader over the deaf is that he/she has had complete exposure to the world of natural spoken language. From birth, the blind child has listened to the real world of sounds and meanings. This small fact should remind us how different are the perceptual worlds of the visual modalities and the linguistic world of human communication. That the blind person can competently access written material either through touch or ear reveals a language function that is basically unimpaired even without the powerful assistance of the visual organ.

The situation is wholly different for the classically deaf person, that child whose auditory function *alone* is disabled. (We are not speaking here of what is increasingly common today, the "multiply-handicapped deaf child.") Deafness brings about not only insuperable problems in the area of reading, but also in general language function. Today teachers of reading in schools for the deaf view language development as one of their most important tasks. Out of this, learning to read becomes a subheading.

Deafness, like blindness, is a disability with subtle gradations. Totally or profoundly deaf children (often born deaf) suffer the most traumatic language impairment. Even a small amount of residual hearing goes a long way toward improving language function, and thus eventually reading. By late adolescence, youngsters having deep hearing problems reach a reading level on average of around fourth grade. Some schools for the deaf that have intensive and almost individualized training claim to do better than this.

The problem for deaf children only begins once the literal levels of reading are achieved—object identification, the concrete modes of expression. The more subtle forms of linguistic expression, either of the literary sort (metaphor) or the relational cognitive subject matters, are difficult for them to grasp. There is a flatness to the average deaf child's understanding of the world—even for a deaf child with good innate intelligence—that is derived from the lack of intellectual development that the natural spoken language could have provided. Later on, this lack affects competency in written expression. Grammatical and syntactical subtletly becomes helplessly complicated, either in reading or writing, because it is often beyond the experiential plane of the child's silent world.

What is interesting in the problem of deafness is the extent to which the natural language forms that essential foundation for later intellectual growth. In the case of the deaf child, a vast structure of modes of thought—characterization of emotion, nuances of expressivity, subtle logical (beyond the visual) relationships—have not been prepared for in the hearing of the spoken language. The close spatial alignment of auditory perception with the language areas of the brain partially explain the subsequent deprivation in language ability that occurs as a result of deafness. It tells us, indirectly, much about the evolutionary course of human development and the dependent variable character of audition, language, and intellectual competency.

Interestingly, because the auditory mode, language ability, and intelligence are three separate dimensions of brain function, even if closely related structurally, certain puzzling situations occur. Occasionally we find among children who have equal levels of deafness and are close in intellectual potential, one child with surprisingly good language facility. There may be no simple environmental explanation, e.g., supportive parents or an extraordinary teacher at some point in the child's development. Simply, the child has unusual innate linguistic facility that shows up in the reading and written work.

The example of deafness gives us a real appreciation of the intimate relationship that hearing and language play in the evolving humanity of the child. It is a relationship that harkens back many millions of years to the origins of the hominids. As one wise man put it, "were I to lose any sense organ, I pray that it not be my hearing. It is through hearing that the essence of my individuality and humanity are given life. In hearing, I gain entrance to the circle of sociality."

Dyslexia and Integrational Disabilities

There was a time when teachers had a ready explanation of a child's difficulties with reading. They rummaged around in family and environment to find those emotional situations that might disturb the learning equilibrium of the poor reader. Often they found that the child was upset. They also often discovered evidence of such family and social causes that explained *to them* this learning failure.

However, as research into this area began to be systematic, disconcerting and contradictory information came to light. Many failing readers had stable backgrounds. Often, disastrous family environments motivated a child to lose himself in his books and read like a house afire. Simply, one could not predict that a poor environment was going to lead first to emotional tensions in the child and then reading failure.

Recent research into genetics as related to learning problems in general gradually turned the equation around. There was no question that in the post-World War II period the correlation of emotional problems and reading failures could be established. However, the causal explanation started to be reversed. Now, reading frustration came first, emotional problems invariably following.

We have learned much about individual differences in children and the fragility of the neurological substructures that are now presumed to be the source both of individual skills and deficiencies. The power of literacy today to make or unmake one's destiny has evoked concern anew about this relationship. We can say with truth that a reading disability, not spotted or subjected to remedial intervention, will inevitably cause emotional problems in the child. It is caused by more than merely the pride in not wanting to be called "stupid." It is the general awareness of capacity and competency in others, followed by frustration over this unknown blockage. All this while other children succeed. The psycho-

140

logical techniques of self-deception to hide the truth, to transfer personal efforts to other behaviors, as reactions to an unknown and incomprehensible barrier, can shatter a child's
equilibrium.

The rationale for readiness programs lies as much in the
opportunity to diagnose possible disabilities before they tor-
pedo the child's confidence as it does in any substantive educational learnings that a child can gain before the age of six.
Developmental rates of children very enormously in these
early years. Thus it is wise to hold some children back until a
later maturational stage has been achieved. The problem of
"educational" maturation or uneven development does not
lie with intellectual or even perceptual maturity. For, the
young child at six is intellectually far beyond any reading material that he/she will be asked to read.

The nub of the problem lies at the integrational level,
that middle area between input of sensory information and
the concluding intellectual phase of understanding. The recognition that the brain is a maze of functions and structures
somehow heaped together in an unknowing human mind
goes back to the end of the nineteenth century. The variety of
head wounds that soldiers brought back with them from wars
at a time in medical history when even serious wounds were
now treatable allowed for the first study of the variety of behaviors served by different parts of the brain and the consequent, often pointillistic (tiny) functions lost as a result of
wounds or strokes.

The famous case in the annals of dyslexia—loss of function in reading—was cited by Dejerine in France in 1892. One
of Dejerine's patients had a stroke, but later was able to go
back to work, maintain a normal life. However, though the
patient could write from dictation, he could not read his own
writing. Only if he traced letters with his hands could he recognize them. However, he could recognize letters such as
"RF," the logo for *Republique de France.* Monsieur X died after a second stroke. In the post-mortem examination, De-

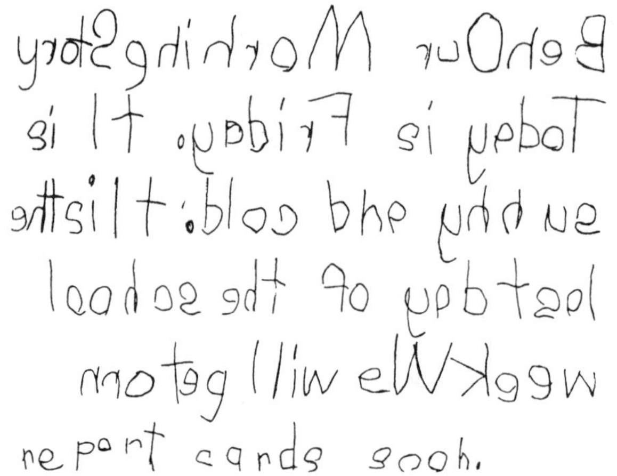

[Mirror-writing handwriting sample:]

BehOur MorhingStory
Today is Friday. It is
sunny and cold. It is the
last day of the school
week We will get our
report cards soon.

This mirror writing was a pupil's first attempt at a writing test. When his teacher pointed out that he had written backwards, he turned the page over and wrote correctly However, whether he was writing backwards or forwards he proved to be dyslexic, reversing his *s,n* and the word *it*.

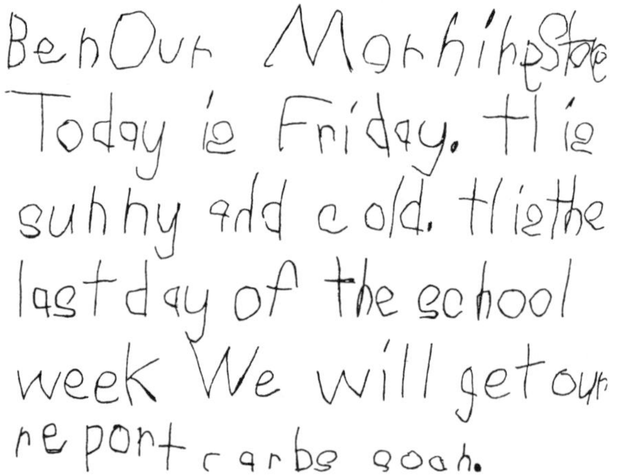

[Handwriting sample:]

BehOur MorhihpStpe
Today is Friday. tl is
suhhy add cold. tl is the
last day of the school
week We will get our
report carbs soah.

Figure 6   Writing-Disabled
(from *How to Recognize and Overcome Dyslexia in Your Child* by Louise Clarke. Courtesy Penguin Books.)

142

lash Monday we wenīt
the Zoo. We spenī much
Time in frunт of an a ~~ī~~
ion cag with hal Seuner
mahgen they made ~~ī~~
us# bulrfe weni wen
They u·g puT ouT they
pours for nuts.

Last Monday we went to the Zoo. We spent much time in front
of an iron cage which held seven monkeys. They made us laugh
when they put out their paws for nuts.

Fig. 10 Writing to dictation. R.G., male aged 11 years. C88584.

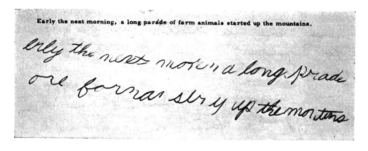

Early the next morning, a long parade of farm animals started up the mountains.

Fig. 11 Writing to dictation. R.S., male aged 13 years.

Jany and Jnely went up the hill to
rzmen a bake for wuner.
Jany wune ane and nerre is line and Jney
gard Susæ fomea

Jack and Jill went up the hill to fetch a pail of water
Jack fell down and broke his crown, and Jill came tumbling after.

Fig. 12 Writing to dictation. J.L., male aged 9 years. C85073.

Figure 7   Dyslexic Children's Writing
     A sample of the writings of dyslexic children.
          (from the *Dyslexic Child* by Macdonald Critchley. Cour-
          tesy Charles C. Thomas.)

143

jerine was able to discover an area on the parietal lobe that had suffered the first blood clot and that presumably affected the patient's reading abilities.

The work of James Hinshelwood, and others a bit later, in the early twentieth century, noted an entire category of nonreaders—subjects who apparently had suffered no explicit damage to the brain while they were growing up. The analysis of the problem of dyslexia was broadened from an analysis of damage to language centers, to a search for developmental lag, or for other environmental explanations for the phenomenon.

The educational implications of dyslexia were first studied in the United States by Samuel Orton in the late 1920's and 30's. Orton called the symptoms he observed in school children "strephosymbolia," twisted symbols. The symptomology of the defect could be seen both in the reading and writing of school-aged children. The writing exhibited many and inconsistent spelling reversals. At times there did not appear to be even a vague similarity between the sounds of words and the way the children spelled them. In reading, normal left-to-right sequences could not be stabilized. It was almost as if the letters bounced around. Writing was often similar to the reading patterns, in that perceptual/motor and small muscle skills were chaotic.

Orton noticed that many of these children did not have strong laterality preferences. They used left and right hands interchangeably for various activities. He thus conjectured that in the absence of certifiable brain damage through accident or stroke, such children had not neurologically matured to the point of having a defined handedness. He concluded that "strephosymbolia" was a product of such a delayed maturation in the brain, suggesting that reading instruction should be put off until the child began to show clear lateral preference.

Today we are much more aware of laterality and its roots in what we call cerebral dominance—the role that each of the hemispheres of the brain plays in establishing not only handedness but the integration of spatial/visual factors normally associated with the right hemisphere, with the major language areas normally centered in the left hemisphere. In the twenties, Orton was still making an educated guess at a time most professional opinion maintained that reading disabilities resulted from emotional traumas caused by special social environmental factors.

Orton was thus virtually alone in assigning these problems to physical, constitutional, and thus developmental factors that were mostly out of the control of the environment. Today a large international organization, *The Orton Society*, is devoted to the study of learning disabilities. Orton's prophetic genetic and developmental insights have been confirmed through myriad cases. Again we have here the tragedy of ideology and dogma of a sociopolitical nature having obscured the traditional good sense of so many wise educators.

Much new information has modified Orton's concentration on laterality. The so-called Gerstmann's syndrome, also noted in the mid-twenties, indicated that the laterality confusion was part of a larger inability of such patients to differentiate parts within the whole, sequences of fingers on the hand, left or right in terms of body image. This confusion extended to the arrangement of letters in the word and the place of single digits in multidigit numbers.

The evidence today argues that in all of us laterality is present from birth, but that its full development or realization in the child can be inhibited by a variety of causes—genetic, perinatal insults, birth trauma, sometimes, as in other dyslexic symptomology, by a retardation in development of the fatty insulation around the neurological pathways in the language areas of the brain. In the beginning of the century, Paul Flechsig had proposed the name "myelination" to describe this insulating material that kept the "neurological current" from sparking and thus short-circuiting the conveying of information. (Keeney and Keeney, 1968, p. 15)

Many dyslectics "grow out of their problem" around puberty. The myelination process, it has been hypothesized, has now taken place to make reading and writing more possible. On the other hand, many of these children overcome the specific functional blockage by finding other means to access deep structure from the reading material. (Joseph Wepman)

Teachers and parents usually observe only the grossest symptoms and expressions of their children's reading difficulties. The exact nature of the "dyslexic" handicap that we see from the outside will probably never be clearly known to us. Thus an outsider would be stumped to prescribe the exact pathway that the learner might use to get around the integrational blockade.

As Joseph Wepman has stated, in dealing with such problems, one never directs one's attention toward remedying the defect. Rather, find and develop whatever modality that will work in realizing the goals of comprehension. So much frustrating remedial reading instruction has been concentrated on "improving" the obvious surface defect, with little realization that often those problems are constitutional and therefore irremediable. The results of such instruction are predictable.

What makes any discussion of these dyslexic types of reading disabilities a chorus of qualifications is the fact that each of the symptoms mentioned above can be subdivided. Thus a child handicapped in reading words might not have trouble with numbers spatially arranged. Perceptual/motor deficiencies in lateral physical relationships might not cause reading difficulties for some children. Some children might not be able to write from dictation but could read and copy. There are cases where dyslexic confusions were rooted in reading English whereas reading a foreign language caused no difficulties.

Thus the same kind of bizarre fragmentation of defects noted in speech and perceptual function also inhabits dyslectics. Of course the problems we note in the visual performance areas can be duplicated in auditory functions. Some children cannot follow oral directions, but are perfectly able to follow written directions. Others cannot hear sounds, yet they can read in an alphabetic language.

General intellectual capacity is often not affected by such learning disabilities. Further, many children with reading disabilities have high general intelligence. In fact, according to one popular argument, dyslectics as a group are of higher than average intelligence. Naturally, the defect has to be moderate in nature. Seriously impaired children may never fully overcome their integrational handicap and thus may never gain full access to deep-structured intellectual competence.

The only reasonable explanation for this is that general intelligence, being dependent on brain size and structure, is relatively unaffected by local developmental lags or traumas that short-circuit the given involved areas. Perhaps, also—and this is hypothetical—individuals of extremely high intelligence may be more vulnerable to either minor or major irregularities in physical function. (Norman Geschwind has argued this for mathematically precocious males.) This kind of relationship reveals itself most clearly in sensitive performing areas such as language.

We can note a number of other odd statistical correlations with such reading disabilities. First, disproportionate numbers of dyslectic children are left-handed. Left-handers are a distinct minority of the population, about ten percent. In theory, these left-handers should have their language areas in the right hemisphere. This is true, however, for only about half the left-handers. Most of the others have it where right-handers do, in the left hemisphere. Fifteen percent of left-handers have language areas in both hemispheres; two percent of right-handers have their language areas in both hemispheres.

Thomas Bever has conjectured that many of the left-handers who have language and reading problems are really right-handers who either prenatally, at birth, or shortly after, suffered some brain trauma in the left hemisphere, resulting in a spontaneous shift of function to the right hemisphere. They have thus become left-handed. (See Kinsbourne and Hiscock, 1978, pp. 169-222.)

A disproportionate number of dyslectics are male. The ratio has been variously estimated at between two-to-one to ten-to-one male/female. Since it is well known that males are more vulnerable physically than females (e.g., birth-death rates), this comes as no surprise. Comparing the developmental progress of males and females reveals the supremacy of females even in reading ability in the early years, and a continued edge in overall linguistic and literary affinities.

The genetic etiology of dyslexia has been fairly well established. A suspiciously large proportion of dyslectics—especially revealed in twin studies—shows a history of dyslexia among close blood relatives. Environmental explanations seem to have weakened as research has continued over the years, with the exception of specific incidents of trauma and brain damage. One should consider both personal as well as family history in making a diagnostic analysis of a child with a severe reading disability. There is too much evidence that shows genetic as well as specific physical environmental causes.

Several conclusions mandate our attention in this brief survey of the integrational dyslexic type of disabled reader: 1. Integrationally disabled children often have superior intelligence and the defect is at no point an indication of intellectual deficiency. 2. Integrational disabilities can range from minute problems, often developmental in origin, and thus of a passing nature, to global performance dysfunctions that can lead to a general hindering of learning. 3. The percentage of dyslexic-type disabled readers and writers ranges from estimates of ten percent of the population to upwards of thirty percent. The larger estimate derives from approximations of general intelligence as compared with reading scores. Often we find individuals significantly retarded in language skill development as compared to their apparent intellectual potential. On this basis of analysis alone, the percentage of the reading-disabled could rise even higher than thirty percent.

4. The complexity of these kinds of reading disabilities argues for early detection (reading readiness programs) and rapid diagnosis, when discovered, by highly specialized authorities. Often, school personnel do not have the medical training or equipment to diagnose properly and then to prescribe proper remediation approaches.

The Slow Reader

Let us consider the cases of three children given a battery of tests, including general I.Q. and reading tests. The results for each of the three children are as follows: Child A: chronological age 10, mental age 10, reading age 13. Child B: chronological age 10, mental age 10, reading age 7. Child C: chronological age 10, mental age 8, reading age 8.

Child A presents an exhilarating anomaly, a child of seemingly average intelligence, whose reading skills and comprehension appear to be far beyond age or intellectual level. This is a child that needs close scrutiny and especially careful retesting. This may be a child with real possibilities, one who could have been overlooked because of relatively mediocre in-school test scores.

Child B seems to be a candidate for our reading disabilities testing program. As suggested above, the school system should utilize its own specialists, but the parents should also be alerted that this child, of seemingly average intelligence, is far behind in reading. A warning light in this case.

Child C is a classic slow learner who is also a slow reader. Since the intelligence and reading scores coincide, both being two grade levels below chronological age, we ought not be alarmed. This child deserves careful teaching, diagnosis, and whatever remediation might be fruitfully applied. With warm encouragement and disciplined teaching, this child might give us a surprise. Many a "dark horse" intellect, obscured from view for a variety of reasons, needed to be discovered by a discerning and insistent teacher.

Careful analysis of a slow reader's performance may reveal that all systems are operative, yet little reading progress is made from week to week. The child's vocabulary will not grow. Neither speed of reading nor quickness of comprehension can be noted from a variety of reading material. When discussion of stories or more factual reading subject matter is undertaken in class, the slow reader will contribute few novel insights into character or motivation. Nor will the child put forth probable outlines of stories or events that are insightful or imaginative, yet reasonable.

Interestingly, in a recent nationwide study of thousands of children, listening comprehension in fifth grade was the best predictor of a range of performance, aptitude, and achievement measures in high school. Thus there are many ways that children's general academic potential can be evaluated and compared with their reading achievements. (Humphreys, 1983)

Psychologists have referred to individuals with limited intelligence as having a concrete as compared to a theoretical mentality. These individuals do well in associative forms of thought or utilizing rote memory patterns of thinking. Rarely will the slow learner be able to leave the here-and-now of given events to entertain logical or hypothetical possibilities based on an assessment of facts.

Fluent reading comprehension is predicated upon one's ability to predict the way through the featural reading material. Slow learners by contrast inevitably display halting, effortful skills. They are not able to predict the probable end of the sentence or get the gist of a half-finished paragraph. The slow learner, relative to his intellectually able reading compatriot, is handicapped, and probably, sadly, irremediably.

We do not mean to imply that slow learners cannot be educated. Rather the type of reading instruction and education in general for such readers must be geared to expecting performance of clearly delineated tasks, what we commonly think of as modest skills, usually preprogrammed activities. Unfortunately, the number of such productive jobs in society is waning.

Every human being deserves to have his/her potentialities fully tapped by the available educational means. There is a program of reading instruction that could help each child do just that. Often we allow unrealistic expectations to dampen our zeal when a student does not quickly succeed. By realizing that there are slow learners who are capable of learning to read, even if on only a modest level of speed and comprehension, we can make the realistic effort.

FURTHER READINGS

Bos, C. S. and R. J. Tierney. (1984) "Inferential reading abilities of mildly retarded and non-retarded students." *American Journal of Mental Deficiency.* Vol. 89, No. 1, 75-82.

Chall, J. S. and A. F. Mirsky, eds. (1978) *Education and the brain.* Chicago: University of Chicago Press.

Ewoldt, C. (1981) "A psycholinguistic description of educated deaf children reading in Sign Language." *Reading Research Quarterly.* No. 1, 58-89.

Gerstmann, J. (1958) "Psychological and phenomenological aspects of disorders of the body image." *Journal of Nervous and Mental Disease.* Vol. 126, 499-512.

Geschwind, N. (1982) "Report on research." *Science.* Vol. 217, 144.

Hinshelwood, J. (1917) *Congenital word-blindness.* London: H. K. Lewis.

Humphreys, L. G. (1983) *Anticipation of gains in general information (Technical rep. No. 282).* Urbana: University of Illinois, Center for the Study of Reading.

Keeney, A. H. and V. T. Keeney, eds. (1968) *Dyslexia.* St. Louis: The C. V. Mosby Company.

Kinsbourne, M. and M. Hiscock. (1978) "Cerebral lateralization and cognitive development", in *Education and the brain.,* ed. by J. Chall and A. Mirsky. Chicago: University of Chicago Press.

Kirk, S. et al. (1978) *Teaching reading to slow and disabled learners.* Boston: Houghton Mifflin.

Leong, Che Kan. (1980) "Laterality and reading proficiency in children." *Reading Research Quarterly.* No. 2, 185-202.

Money, John, ed. (1966) *The disabled reader: Education of the dyslexic child.* Baltimore: Johns Hopkins Press.

Moores, D. F. (1970) "Psycholinguistics and deafness." *American Annals of the Deaf.* January, 37-48.

Orton, S. (1937) *Reading, writing and speech problems in children.* New York: W. W. Norton.

Stevenson, H. W. et al. (1982) "Reading disabilities: The case of the Chinese, Japanese, and English." *Child Development.* Vol. 53, 1164-1181.

PART III

Educational Pathways

11

The Program

Tradition and Knowledge

TO BE BOTH logical and practical, a reading program should be a direct outgrowth of what we know about how children learn to read. The problem has been that we know so little beyond the lore of well-experienced teachers who always seemed to wend their way over and around the obstacles and get the job done. It is no longer a matter of finding this old pro of a teacher, surrounding her with ten or twelve eager youngsters, a pile of simple books, some paper, pencils, perhaps chalk and blackboard, and saying "go to it."

To a great extent we have inherited that way of teaching from the Romans; up until the nineteenth century we had improved little on it. Since the nineteenth century, tradition has given way to science and knowledge. All well and good. However, explicit human efforts imply a philosophy that defines progress, science, and knowledge. Here we get deeply involved in value issues, which often translate themselves into the political arena, to patriotic groups, professional associations, state public schools regulators, and local boards of education. Too often the reading program has become subjected to such a "can of political worms."

The opportunity for educators and public alike in the psycholinguistic tradition of reading research and application is that there are no old political vested interest groups. The only intellectual opposition comes from the behavioristic psychological traditions. Although the preeminent representative, B. F. Skinner, is a great figure, outside academia his work in education has elicited little public agitation, and often disdain.

What one does in a reading program that begins in kindergarten is to keep clearly in mind the long-term objectives of such schooling, starting at the point where the child nears the readiness mark. Then one looks carefully at the developmental, intellectual, even social patterns as the child progresses through the grades to make sure that methods and programs coincide, and, most important, shift the point of instruction along with these patterns.

In the next chapter we will discuss the issue of teaching methods, which is a separate concern as compared with the actual progression of curriculum materials in reading that are designed for school use. Too often the program has immersed itself in method or vice versa. The result is that our words tend to have little relevance to the concrete problems. Of course, we lose effective purpose here, i.e., we don't know what we're talking about, we use jargon, and thus we can't educate effectively.

A reading program, therefore, is the concrete outgrowth or embodiment of a theory as to how children learn to read and the long-term purposes of reading in the educational and social world in which they will grow to maturity. Teaching method is the actual "how to" bring this purpose in the reading program to fruition. In this chapter, we will be talking about the plan of the reading program, the kinds of curriculum (reading) materials we will develop in coordination with the overall language arts program. Naturally the scientific and conceptual understanding comes first.

Next come the readers for the children. In the eighteenth and nineteenth centuries, the readers, in addition to reflecting the religious and cultural values of the various communities, maintained the tradition of introducing the letters with their most common word/phonic examples, e.g., *The New England Primer*, "In Adams *fall* we sinned *all*." One could hardly argue that systematic phonics or decoding instruction inhered in these books. Rather it was assumed that those for whom schooling and literacy were to be a pathway to the adult vocations would easily combine the few letter/phoneme clues with their word exemplifications, and make the inductive jump into gradual fluent reading competency.

In other words, the children would be given a number of letter/sound correspondences as illustrated in common words. The children would then be expected after some drill and memorization to absorb spontaneously all the "rules and exceptions" and create their own "dictionary" of rules. A little bit of phonics instruction would go a long way. For those students having great difficulty, apprenticeship in the mechanical arts would be suggested as an alternate route to adult vocational competency. Naturally it was hoped that these children would gain some literacy in time, perhaps through a process of osmosis! Remember, compulsory education laws were instituted only in the latter part of the nineteenth century.

It is from this period, the last decades of the nineteenth and the early decades of the twentieth century that we see a new kind of national reading series. The Boyden-Elson ——▶ (Scott-Foresman Readers (1897)); McGuffey ——▶ (American Book Readers (1890's)); and the Riverside ——▶ (Houghton Mifflin Readers (1910)) predict the trend of things to come. Gradually, these became what we call basal readers, a series of carefully graded books with a growing percentage of ancillary materials, workbooks, supplemental readers, and the like.

It is important to keep separate the concept of the basal reader from the reading program per se. These basal readers, which quickly took over reading pedagogy, had a content within their covers. The idea was to minimize the failure rate in a growing population of children, often just off the boat, from the four corners of the world. These basal readers contained within themselves a wide variety of materials in the language arts, not merely the old morality stories of the early readers, that were then followed by a few questions on comprehension.

The key element in the reading program purveyed by the basal was increasingly a basic sight vocabulary of words quickly and easily recognized that would start the child on the road to comprehension. Early in our century, the results of Cattell's tachistoscope experiments were now being applied within the basal readers, which in turn now became part of the teaching methods resources of the profession.

The look-say/sight approach to reading became almost synonymous with the basal series. They did not need to be so identified. As we will point out shortly, basals could be given a highly phonics "linguistic" and decoding orientation. However, until the 1960's, the look-say/sight vocabulary approach dominated the philosophy of most American reading programs.

As we noted earlier, the look-say/sight approach reached its peak of use in the 1930's and 1940's, coinciding with the maturing of the progressive era in education, the project method, the experience curriculum. By the late 1950's and early 60's, goaded in part by the Soviet challenge to American technological and military domination, the entire public educational enterprise came under serious scrutiny.

Conservatives, who identified "progressives" in any form with political liberals, began to examine the results of almost two generations of the dominance of the look-say/

sight-word reading approach. The diminution of standards observable in the reading basals series themselves did point to an unexpected problem. Somehow a monkey wrench had been slipped into the smooth working machinery of the orthodox reading program.

Something dreadful had happened. Attribute it, for example, to the failure of a reading program to fulfill its educational promises because of its inner weakness. Perhaps the look-say approach was mistaken in its basic assumptions about how humans learn to read.

In the thirty years between 1930 and 1960, the United States had added almost sixty million people, from about 120 million to 180 million. The consciousness of success or failure in reading was certainly heightened. We could no longer send our illiterates out into the "mechanical trades." Also to be taken into consideration was the fact that progressive education in its orientation was not overly subject-matter oriented. Many teachers were trained to believe that individuality and social adjustment, interest motivation, and just plain old happiness were more important for the child than systematic instruction in a subject matter. Unfortunately, literacy in a new era, with the addition of television to the cultural scene, required far more intensive commitment to the complex abstractions of written language and mathematics than in a less distracting world.

Phonics/Linguistics Programs

The growing realization that all was not well in the programming of reading instruction led to an increase in phonics instruction in all basal revisions by the early 1960's. In addition, the growing debate over the nature of language and the study of linguistics led to some real diversification in philosophy and program in reading. We must remember that the 60's were years of economic and demographic expansion. The chances that a new approach to reading would attract an audience of interested public school districts were high. In fact, the stakes in the competitive publishing industry were enormous. The success of a relatively small publisher in winning Louisiana and Texas to its K-6 basal reading series for five years literally made one senior author, an acquaintance of this writer, an extremely wealthy professor.

Thus was born the phonics/linguistic approach to reading. This approach resulted in a series of basal readers, which emanated from several publishers, undergirded by a quite different philosophy of the reading process. Distinguished scholars such as Leonard Bloomfield, Charles Fries, and Charles Walcutt had been arguing forcefully that the underlying elements out of which language was built were the distinctive sounds of the spoken language.

These sounds, as built into the written English language with all its irregular spelling usages, still constituted the stuff of reading. The breaking of the visual written code into its auditory components would result in reading success. The theory was that in a sense the whole-word approach to reading skipped over an entire sequence of learnings that the children needed to make before they could build the visual form of the spoken language into meaningful units.

What the researchers implied was that for some children with extraordinarily good auditory/visual receptors, a very few clues might bring about an almost immediate jump to grasping the sound-to-sight relationship of other written symbols to their spoken equivalents. In reality, these children were moving beyond the decoding-to-sound process with extraordinary speed. Their immediate grasping of the shape and meaning of a word as a whole was only an appearance. Hidden in this process was a surreptitious breaking of the sight-to-sound code that preceded "whole"-word identification.

160

Unfortunately, these young virtuosi were few and far between. Most children would become reading failures without careful phonics/linguistic decoding to sound followed by having these "sound bricks" built into a structure of words and meanings. The look-say/whole-word method, because it violated our natural method of learning language, thereby failed most children in their attempts to learn to read.

Further support for this new turn in reading programming came from Jeanne Chall's book, *Learning to Read: the great debate* (1967, 1983), discussed in Chapter 3. Funded by the Carnegie Foundation, which sought an ecumenical solution to the reading wars of the fifties and sixties, Chall came down on the side of a decoding emphasis (phonics/linguistics). While her survey did not end the debate, it gave additional impetus for the new programs.

Lippincott and Merrill were the two publishers who now entered the fray. Of the two, Merrill was the most radical, taking its cue from the somewhat behavioristic linguistic school of Bloomfield and Fries. Sounds were introduced one at a time in easily recognized words. However, the words were only the vehicles to develop brick-by-brick a repertoire of sight-to-hearing sounds that would subsequently be recognized by the child in other reading contexts.

Only after a large enough repertoire of sounds could be decoded from the visual print could the child confidently face new words. Hidden in those written symbols was their true inner reality, the sounds of our spoken language. Drill in sound recognition was to be the key to releasing the meaning hidden in the written language.

So committed were the Merrill authors to this notion of drill in sound recognition that they chose an extremely radical path for their basal reader. It was not enough that the stories sounded like amateur doggerel, so annoyingly onomatopoetic in their repetitions of sounds, and seemingly so non-contextual just to provide the proper drill. But, all illustrations were eliminated. Just plain white pages with black markings. Why?

The answer was clear and simple. In the traditional Scott-Foresman-type look-say reader, the illustrations often illuminated the story as specifically as did the words on the page. The child, after reading the "whole words" silently, would be asked comprehension questions from the teacher's manual. The questions would be answered correctly and insightfully. Yet too often these children could read barely a word on the page. Too much context, some critics charged.

Obviously, basal illustrations were proving counterproductive. The vocabulary may have been restrictive here in the Merrill readers, but at the least, the authors were responding to the challenge of the times with a real alternative. Moreover, this program had powerful support from noted scholars in the discipline of linguistics.

Lippincott's program, authored by Glen McCracken and Charles Walcutt, was somewhat less radical. Lippincott's *Basic Reading* program when issued in 1963 and 1969 preempted the expected criticism of Merrill's severe reading discipline. It had plenty of illustrations. Most interestingly, it attempted an end run around Merrill by expanding the vocabulary to fit the need for more words to exemplify the particular sound being taught.

In the meantime, its establishment rival, Scott-Foresman's *The New Basic Readers* (1962) had itself fudged from its rigorous whole-word recognition bias by adding phonics exercises in the respective workbooks that accompanied the basals. It even expanded its highly restricted vocabulary to accommodate a greater emphasis on sounds to be taught along with the word tests that required mastery. Yet the Scott-Foresman and other traditional basals did not vary enough to alter the patterns of teacher training for the future.

A comparison of these two watershed reading text series is interesting. Unfortunately, subsequent social and educational events made the contest moot since the eyes and ears of educators and public were soon elsewhere. On the other hand, it was clear from the comparative impact of the innovative Lippincott program what the successes and failures consisted in.

Examining the preprimer and primer equivalents of first grade instruction gives us a sense of the divergence of curricular philosophies. Scott-Foresman offered seventy-nine new and different words in 183 pages, somewhat of an improvement over their 1952 program. Lippincott, on the other hand, exposed the first graders to a whopping 483 words in only seventy-eight pages. (Note that the concept "page" is important for young children since it is the focus of their learning attention. The print must be fairly large in size, the page fairly small to handle.)

Lippincott introduced thirty-three new words for every one hundred words to which the children were exposed. In Scott-Foresman, only two words in every hundred would be new. Thus Lippincott's vocabulary was one of extremely *low* redundancy—seventy-four percent of the words were *not* repeated in the following several pages. Scott-Foresman, by contrast, repeated eighty percent of its words in the following pages, extremely *high* redundancy.

What Lippincott had attempted to do in extending the vocabulary was to buffer the immense load of new words by making them phonetically regular. Thus, immediately following its introduction, each new phonic element to be taught was repeated in a minimum of three of the six new words and on one occasion in forty-eight new words on the next page or two. The theory here is that the new words would be easy to identify or understand because they emphasized a familiar phonic element: a long "a" or a hard "c," or the "ch" sound, as in "church." "Rags got the water off" is one sample sentence emphasizing hard "g," short "a."

Scott-Foresman by contrast introduced the basic forty-six to fifty phonic/grapheme elements in a mostly random

f sound of ph

photograph telephone elephant nephew
pharmacy Philip pamphlet orphan
phonograph telegraph phantom Ralph
Phyllis autograph

hard ch

character chemistry chemical chemist
chorus Christmas chrome school
scholar ache stomach echo scheme
schooner anchor orchestra

 sh sound of ch

Chicago machine chute Charlotte

Figure 8 The Phonics/Linguistic System
The phonics/linguistic approach to primary reading.
(from *Lippincott's Basic Reading* by McCracken and Walcutt. Courtesy J. P. Lippincott.)

164

A Funny Christmas Present

Philip Anderson lived on Spring Street in a small town called Andover. He was seven years old.

Philip had a little sister. Her name was Phyllis. Phyllis was five years old.

On Christmas morning Philip and Phyllis came running downstairs. They were very excited because they wanted

Billy's Picture

Miss Day said, "Now it is fun time.
What do you want to do, children?"

"Let's make pictures," said Jane.
"That is fun."

"Oh, yes!" said the boys and girls.

Miss Day said, "All right, children.
Get what you want for your pictures."

Figure 9   A Look-Say Reading Text
A typical look-say/whole-word lesson.
(from *More Fun With Our Friends* by Helen M. Robinson,
Marion Monroe, A. S. Artley. Courtesy Scott-Foresman).

166

Jane said, "Here, Susan.
Blue is a pretty color.
Do you want blue?"

"Yes, thank you," said Susan.
"I can make a bird with that color.
Birds are easy to make."

Billy March said, "Please let me
have all the colors, Jane.
I am going to make a funny picture."

All the children got colors.
Then they began to work.

manner. Rarely were they repeated in the immediate vicinity. The Scott-Foresman philosophy was affirmed: "A child learns a word only by seeing it many times. . . . The act of reading becomes interpretation from the day a child holds his first pre-primer in his hands." Clearly interpretation was to be developed from an extremely small vocabulary, with high repetition, which for the eager proto-fluent reading child could hardly have been other than deadening.

	No. of pages in book	New words introduced	New words per running 100 words	% of new words repeated on following page	Phonic elements
Scott-Foresman (1962)	183	79	2	80%	Rarely repeated immediately
Lippincott (1969)	78	483	33	26%	Repeated in most new words

Lippincott's teacher's edition of *Basic Reading* (1969) stated it clearly also: "Instead of vocabulary control in terms of word frequency we use phoneme/grapheme (i.e., sound-spelling) control in terms of simplicity and regularity." It is true that Lippincott did concentrate on sound spelling controls, with enormous redundancy of the same forty-six to fifty phonic elements that Scott-Foresman so casually introduced. However, the price of this heavy emphasis on learning the sounds and their spelled equivalents was an enormous vocabulary load in stories that were often strained and awkward because of attempts to find words that fit the particular phonic elements being taught.

The outcomes are interesting. The early sixties represent the nadir of Scott-Foresman leadership. Other publishers, Ginn, Houghton Mifflin, for instance, were introducing a grab bag of new reading tricks to woo the education profession. Innumerable beginning reading methods, in addition to I.T.A. appeared—*Rebus, Words in Color,* etc. Attacks on sight-word reading from all directions, including the new linguistics, pushed Scott-Foresman, at least temporarily, into the background to wait out the storm.

As for Lippincott's phonics/linguistic approach, it was virtually a disaster. The oddness of the stories was already a minor put-off both for children and teachers. The vocabulary load was too much. The few children who could cope certainly didn't need the fallacious assistance of so-called phonics regularities. The slow readers faltered, for readers for the reading-disabled needed much more specialized and graded materials. Thus Lippincott gradually toned down the rigorousness of its phonics/linguistic commitment, reduced its vocabulary load, and made over its entire basal program into a format not inconsistent with most of the middle-of-the-road "meaning"-centered series of the 1980's.

One surprising result of this contest of philosophies was that the Merrill series of Bloomfield and Fries, which eschewed any compromise at least for the primary grades, did make headway. However, now it was useful to the specialized reader, the slow or visually-disabled reader. For those children who needed much drilling in mediated reading to make even a stab at comprehension, Merrill readers were useful. For perceptual-visual-integrationally handicapped readers, the concentration on phonics elements, the large print, and slow pace were helpful. At least, here, a measure of mediated reading comprehension could take place through a sequential nondemanding sound/grapheme-oriented program.

run   runs

gun   guns

bun   buns

fun

sun

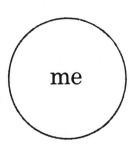

Figure 10   A Linguistic Reader Drill
Phonic drill without pictures.
(from *Merrill Linguistic Readers* by Charles C. Fries et al.
Courtesy Charles E. Merrill Books.)

Not in the Sun!

"Pam, run and tag me.
It's fun," said Dan.

"It's not fun in the sun,"
said Pam.

Pam sits at the fan,
and Dan runs to Jim.

"It's not fun to run
in the sun," said Jim.

Dan runs to Dad.
"Not in the sun!" said Dad.

Psycholinguistics and Reform

Throughout the seventies, the impact of psycholinguistics on the field of reading was palpable. Psycholinguistic theory did not mandate any particular stance in reading instruction, except for its great emphasis on fluent reading for meaning. It certainly raised serious questions about the advisability of developing a basal series through the phonics/linguistic approach. Nevertheless, the political popularity of this so-called phonics, conservative, back-to-basics association continued to sell these emphases.

Joining Lippincott and Merrill were Allyn and Bacon and the Laidlaw publishing companies, which stressed a heavy explicit phonics beginning to their programs. In general, this group buffered the starkness of their program by adding a strong meaning and skill development element from second and third grade on. In a sense, they recognized that the so-called phonics/linguistic element was truly a mediated reading approach that had to be followed more intellectually, less mechanically with comprehension skills.

In fact, the Merrill readers from the fourth grade on made a 90° turn, switching radically to a rich skill, comprehension, and literature orientation. This again underlies the empty theoretical basis of these phonics programs. One wonders what educational rationale allows publishers and schools to destroy potentially able readers in the first three grades, then suddenly to throw at them a conceptual reading fare for which there is little preparation. Further, for the halting, perhaps disabled reader, the transition from "man, fan, ban" to the meaning complexities of a full middle grade program must be overwhelming.

Of all the publishers, Scott-Foresman made the most intensive efforts to absorb the psycholinguistic ideas, recruiting a stellar list (K. Goodman, J. Wepman, I. Aaron, J. Manning) of reading authorities as "authors" for their mid-1970's *Read-*

The Program

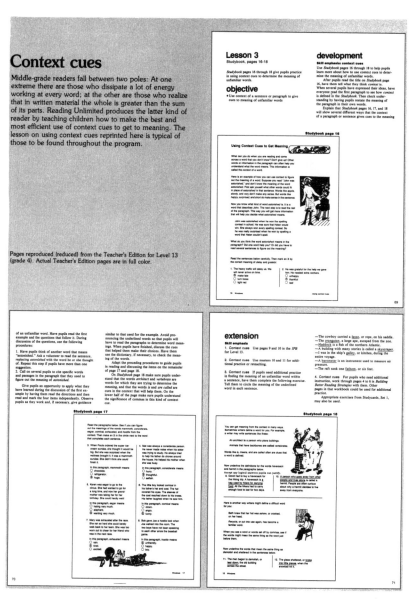

Figure 11   Recent Meaning Emphasis Exercises
Middle grades comprehension skill development in a recent basal modernization.

(from *Reading Unlimited K-8* by Ira Aaron et al. Courtesy Scott-Foresman.)

ing Unlimited basals. Scott-Foresman was joined by such stalwarts as Ginn, Laidlaw, and Holt. Here, we note a rich combination of sight words, skill development, comprehension, literature, as well as supplementary phonics instruction intending now to touch all the bases.

With almost three-fourths of a century of experience in teaching children from a vast variety of backgrounds, the publishers have begun to retreat to an eclectic middle ground. In today's reading program, you will find every technique that has ever been successfully employed, and at practically every stage of the reading process. In fact, most school systems choose their reading programs from among the various publishers not on the basis of scientific or philosophical orientation, but on the basis of cost considerations, attractiveness of format, or the available ancillary materials and supplementary programs, i.e., workbooks, variety of reading levels, teachers' edition, special cassette programs.

Common Sense and the Program

It is fair to say that the programmatic aspects of the reading curriculum are in a quiet state. The ferment of the 1960's and 70's is over. The panaceas have disappeared, the controversies have been absorbed into an all-encompassing eclecticism.

As one examines the various reading series put out by the major publishers, it is clear that in their rush to do everything they have crowded their basals and ancillary text materials with a vast hodgepodge of skills and approaches almost as bad as the single-minded "systems" approach that formerly defined the school reading program.

What I would like to do as a conclusion to this chapter is attempt to clarify and explicate what good reading practice might be on the basis of the extension of psycholinguistic theory as I have here presented it. The ironic aspect to what follows, and indeed is true of all reading systems, is that all programmatic values pale next to a truly inspired teacher. The artist/educator, a person for whom a certificate of merit or special pay is really irrelevant, can transmute, literally, dust into pedagogical gold.

A — *Development.* In the preceding chapters, we have attempted to present a pattern of linguistic development in the child as it pertains to reading. Every child is somewhat different; some children will move through these stages in jumps, often irregular pulses of learning. Yet, because English is an alphabetic language, the patterns of learning to read will have to follow their special logic that can lead the student to fluent reading. In that sense, all children become members of the reading club, no matter what speedy or lethargic pace they take, even the detours in learning modality that they must follow temporarily.

It is important that the three distinct stages in a child's reading development be taken into account in all reading programs: readiness, mediated reading, fluent reading.

In readiness, we prepare the ground for a recognition of the relationship of the written alphabet to the natural spoken dialect. We also ought to be alert to any special language and/or reading problems that begin to rear their heads, as well as to recognize the individual learning preferences of the child.

In mediated reading, which can begin for a child as early as kindergarten and first grade, the challenge of phonics instruction must be faced. The auditorially unimpaired child, with good visual integration skills, taught with sensitivity and flexibility, will leap ahead into fluent reading by being able to break the featural code. Here a child will rarely have to decode written words to sound before comprehension takes place.

At any rate, the program should give the teacher a wide variety of phonics/decoding strategies for finding the right key for each child, especially the child that needs mediated reading crutches well into second or third grade. The test in the mediated reading stage of the program is how well it provides materials in decoding that efficiently help the child to abandon this crutch.

Fluent reading is the stage of reading for meaning, comprehension, deepening the child's extraction of knowledge from the written medium. Here, the key must remain the development of skills for thinking in a wide variety of subject matter areas, from analyzing character in short stories to figuring out verbal mathematics problems. No matter how rich and interesting the reading and writing materials are in this stage, it will take truly inspired teachers both pedagogically and intellectually to make a success out of the language program from third grade on.

B — *Variable Learning.* Given that we accept the fact that children have differing powers of intellect, some simply being extraordinarily bright, others slow, we must recognize another, often not evident, fact. Even children with seemingly similar powers of thought have individual valences in their learning styles and thus in their talents and interests.

Why this is so is largely a mystery of the complex brain structure in humans and the diverse genetic elements that go into the creation of an individual human brain. When the environmental factors of family, social and ethnic backgrounds are added, flexibility and variability become the name of the game for a reading and language arts program.

A reading program must be prepared to respect these modalities of learning. (Joseph Wepman) One publisher or one basal series can't possibly fill every bill. In attempting to do so, publishers often hit the median and thus miss most of the children. That is the tragedy of a public school structure that requires a state or city to sign up with one or two publishers to provide for each classroom and each pupil.

176

C — *Meaning, Cognitive Emphasis.* What is the purpose of a reading program? This is the question that must be asked again and again. The answer has to be: to create readers who can independently extract meaning from the material. Reading is one of the ways humans communicate ideas to each other. Thought, cognitive, and logical power to act on experience constitute *one set* of purposes in the reading program. Now, how ought this general and unexceptional goal translate itself into the reading program?

Many educators are beginning to feel there is a too premature emphasis on learning subject matter in the elementary and junior high school grades. Note the flood of information that comes to us through the mass media. Even travel is available to a large proportion of the working and middle classes. Ought the schools build on this advantage in the reading and language arts program? I think not. Such precocity may be illusory. Precocious children often become simply facile flingers of facts.

As we well know, youngsters change enormously in the adolescent years; they experience a literal rebirth of powers, talents, personality. This is where they can be guided in making their transition to adulthood. In early adolescence, fourteen to fifteen years, they gain a peak of intellectual powers. New facts can be built out of such mind skills. The reading program should make youngsters ready for this leap.

This is prelude to arguing that the various elements of the elementary school program, for example, social science and natural science, should not be included for their knowledge or information component. Rather, they should be studied, as is math, to develop the various intellectual skills that will prepare the youngsters for high school and college programs. Here the argument for the strictly basal approach to reading weakens as we approach the middle school grades (5-6). What we need is a wide variety of skill building reading materials.

In short, the focus of reading and the language arts should be to build intellectual power, to strengthen skills of independent learning in this complex symbolic area of written language. It is truly unimportant how much a child knows about dinosaurs, local Indian lore, or the process of photo-synthesis. Much of this learning can be gained later when it is presented in a deeper intellectual context. Going over and over the same materials (dinosaurs, planetary system) at varying stages in the schooling process has turned off too many students. By keeping our eyes on our true educational goals, we can simplify and purify our efforts in reading, rid ourselves of the trivia and concentrate on developing each child's unique power and personality.

D — *The Cultural Dimension.* There is more to the language arts program than "intellectual power." Humans, playing with language, also create literature—fiction, poetry, storytelling. These must always be an important and integral part of a reading program. However, we must separate, even if only in logic, what must be integrated in practice.

Simply, a literature program for youngsters all through the school years while it works with the same language materials—words and sentences—has a somewhat different *purpose* than the conceptual one. Naturally we want to lead our youngsters gradually toward the moment that they will enjoy reading the likes of Shakespeare, Balzac, Keats, Melville. Part of the literacy aspect of the language program will always have as its goal building on the critical, conceptual abilities of the young. Still, there is here an additional concern not merely to create writers of novels and poetry, and thus critics of the literary tradition, but individuals who read for "educated pleasure." The level of reading in this country for these purposes is admittedly scandalously low. Could it be the result partially of not keeping clarity in our purpose in teaching literature, of confusing it with concepts in science?

Whatever the cause of this general decline in our language sensibilities, we need to try to reverse direction. By viewing the intentions of a literature/language program from the standpoint of its differences from the purely skill learnings in reading and language arts in the discursive logical areas, we might be able to broaden the scope of the instruction and discover many more willing minds.

FURTHER READINGS

Aaron, I. E. et al. (1976) *Reading unlimited.* Chicago: Scott-Foresman.

Anderson, R. C. et al., eds. (1984) *Learning to read in American Schools.* Hillsdale, N. J.: Erlbaum.

Bloomfield, L. and C. Barnhart. (1961) *Let's read: A linguistic approach.* Detroit: Wayne State University Press.

Chall, J. S. (1983) *Stages of reading development.* New York: McGraw-Hill.

Durkin, D. (1981) "Reading comprehension instruction in five basal reader series." *Reading Research Quarterly.* November 4, 515-544.

Fries, C. (1963) *Linguistics and reading.* New York: Holt, Rinehart, and Winston.

Fries, C. et al. (1966) *Merrill linguistic readers.* Columbus, Ohio: Charles E. Merrill Books.

Gray, William S. et al. (1957) *Basic reading skills for junior high use.* Chicago: Scott-Foresman and Company.

Levin, H. and J. P. Williams, eds. (1970) *Basic studies in reading.* New York: Basic Books.

McCracken, G. and C. C. Walcutt. (1963) *Lippincott's basic reading.* Philadelphia: J. B. Lippincott.

Osborne, J. et al., eds. (1985) *Reading education: Foundations for a literate America.* Lexington, Mass: Lexington Books.

Robinson, H. M. et al. (1962) *The new basic readers.* Chicago: Scott-Foresman.

12

Teaching Method

Teaching Teachers How to Teach

THE PLACE, Columbia University Teachers College.
Time, a number of years ago. Scene, a large lecture hall during a course in "Elementary Curriculum." The speaker that day, a guest lecturer, a teacher and curriculum supervisor in a New Jersey school district, recent recipient of a doctorate from Columbia.

Subject of lecture, the speaker's experience with individualized reading procedures. She was now an authority on this method of teaching reading. Later, Ms. W., as I will call her, went on to make a fine reputation for herself in the field and would author several books in the area. Her lecture was fascinating, especially to me as a novice teacher.

I remember vividly how animatedly she described her method of preparing the reading and other language arts materials for her twenty-seven pupils. Each child had an individualized program of reading that covered books selected, read, and reported on; the various writing activities were geared to the material read and the child's own developmental status and rate. In addition, there was a heavy emphasis on anecdotal record keeping of the children's progress, occasional testing (individualized), and, of course, reports to the principal and the parents.

My neighbor, who was a stranger to me in that large class, nudged me. "I'm glad it works for Ms. W.'s twenty-seven angels," she whispered, "but let her try it with my twenty-five geniuses. If she's still alive in a week, I'll give her a medal." That was pretty much my own feeling, as I was still struggling with my first teaching experience, of only twenty-three fifth graders. Despite great variability in their academic skills, the children were being taught in reading groups and I was using basal readers, but, I thought, not slavishly.

Ms. W.'s lecture concerned teaching method, the proper organization of the class, and the manner in which a reading program was being presented to the pupils. She rarely discoursed about the underlying philosophy of learning to read that undergirded her work in that second grade class of hers. This was too bad, because teaching method does depend to a certain extent on what one believes to be the manner in which children learn to read.

In a course on the elementary curriculum, one would expect a major emphasis on programmatic matters. As it was, the issues of the reading program—the structure of learning to which the pupils will be subjected—and method—the manner in which the teacher will deal with the interaction of children and curricular materials—were merged in the discusion. The two issues are really logically separate elements in the reading program. Naturally, they can't be separated in the actual teaching process.

However, when viewed as to their essential character, the entire educational process can become clear if we know what we are talking about. For example, one can argue that to teach teachers methods of applying curricular materials to the pupils in a classroom, one would ideally present the

182

novice teachers with real live children in a classroom situation. On the other hand, the study of the reading process and general curricular issues in the school program can be carried out in a more academic environment. One can even here develop some of the hypothetically different approaches in method, of which individualized reading is one, from the standpoint of the nature of the curriculum to be studied. This applies to mathematics, foreign languages, and social studies, as well as to reading.

Only by separating the issue of teaching method from the problem of developing appropriate reading curricular programs can we see the issues proper to each domain. There are some teaching methods that would seem to follow directly from the specific types of reading program that the children are experiencing. Other methods are neutral. We need to be clear about these distinctions.

Method and Program: Distar

An example of the close dependency of method to program is *Distar*. Created by Carl Bereiter and Siegfried Engelmann and published by Science Research Associates of Chicago, *Distar* created controversy in the profession from the start. The authors presented the program as an antidote to the widespread reading failures of the sixties. They concentrated on the beginning reading sequence. The assumption of *Distar* was that the bricks of reading knowledge were contained in the units of grapheme to speech/sound correlations. The child had to learn the written equivalents of spoken words and their component sounds.

There was room for neither chance nor failure. The teacher would drill the children orally until they were programmed to learn. Unlike the Merrill readers, where the focus

Distar® Instructional System

Distar® Reading

> **BASAL FOR PRESCHOOL—GRADE 3**

DISTAR® Reading, part of the DISTAR Instructional System, is made up of three consecutive sections—DISTAR Reading I, II, and III. Each is designed for approximately one year's work. Based on the idea that all students can learn if they are taught in the appropriate way, DISTAR Reading provides basic reading instruction through a structured approach.

Suggested Use Basic reading instruction for children in preschool through grade 3—from the student who has difficulty learning to the average and the bright.

Distar® Reading I

© 1974, 1969

Authors Siegfried Engelmann and Elaine C. Bruner

The Program Distar® Reading I, Second Edition, more efficiently teaches the skills needed to decode words: sound-symbol identification, left-to-right sequence, and oral blending of sounds to make a word. Children then progress to word and later sentence reading. Direct and economical teaching of concepts, followed by immediate response from the group, ensures continuous evaluation and eventual mastery. In-program tests supplement daily evaluation and provide for skipping procedures so that faster learners can skip 40 of the 160 lessons. Beginning comprehension skills are emphasized, in both oral and written exercises.

Highlights Revised formats incorporate teaching techniques improved through five years of experience. All instructions for a lesson are together in one presentation book, including complete directions for teaching stories and seatwork.

- Minimal daily preparation for teachers.
- 20-30 minutes of seatwork per day.
- Reusable story books for the children.
- An optional spelling track.
- Improved Teacher's Guide including detailed teaching instructions.
- Student Take-Homes bound in workbook form.

Components Reading I teacher materials consist of 3 spiral-bound presentation books, a test book, a spelling book, a teacher's edition of the student Take-Home books, copies of the Storybooks, a cassette containing sound pronunciation and sample tasks, a Teacher's Guide, an acetate page protector, and group-progress indicators. Reading I student materials consist of 3 Storybooks and 3 Take-Home books for each child.

DISTAR® Reading I		List Price	School Price
7-8300	DISTAR® Reading I, Teacher Kit	$125.33	$94.00
7-8306	Additional Teacher's Guide	4.00	3.00
7-8320	DISTAR® Reading I Storybooks (set of 3 Storybooks for 1 student)	5.20	3.90
7-8315	DISTAR® Reading I Take-Home Books (set of 3 Take-Home books for 1 student)	5.67	4.25
7-8326	DISTAR® Reading I Sampler Kit	6.60	4.95
7-8319	DISTAR® Reading I Behavioral Objectives	1.15	.85

For a class of 30 students you will need:
1 teacher kit for DISTAR Reading I
30 sets of Storybooks
30 sets of Take-Home books

To order components, see page 134.

Figure 12 The Distar Program
How Distar conceptualizes its program.
(courtesy *Distar Instructional System* by S. Engelmann
and E. C. Bruner, Science Research Associates.)

184

was on the written page, unpictured and slow-paced, *Distar* used choral methods, rote repetition, heavily laden with teacher direction.

No provision was made for a transition into fluent reading. The assumption seemed to be that once the sounds were learned in their visual forms, an automatic transition to word and sentence understanding would take place. Method and drill thus grew out of the strong programmatic assumptions that the clarification of each of the phonic sounds in its written equivalent constituted both the beginning and fulfillment of the reading process. Most educators were appalled at the rote, mechanical, and *un*individualized methodology that lay at the core of the *Distar* program and its methodological realization in the classroom.

What is interesting about *Distar* is its eventual acceptance by a special educational clientele, the inner city preschool and elementary school. Whereas the Merrill readers have found acceptance by educators for children with reading disabilities, *Distar* is being used successfully with the socially and culturally deprived. It may be that the lack of clear spoken English or the lack of normal conversation by elders makes it necessary for these children to hear their language while they are being acquainted with the supposed written equivalents. The lack of an environment stressing personal organization and discipline likewise necessitates the almost army-like regimentation in reading and other basic learning subjects. In any case, one can observe in *Distar* that a conceptualization of the nature of the beginning reading process and its programmatic realization lead to certain untraditional practices in the classroom. Here method follows clearly on the heels of program in reading instruction.

As a general rule, it can be argued that the specialized method—what the teacher actually does to teach and organize the classroom program in reading—applies more often to children having particular needs, those who are handicapped, deprived, perhaps even highly talented and gifted children.

However, in the latter case, many educators would recommend that the teacher for the most part "stay out of the way."

The Basal

Today, as always, the "basal" method of teaching reading is the approach used in an overwhelming number of United States public schools. In the vast majority of public school districts, it is the *mandated* method. Here materials dictate method, for the teacher has to adopt the given publisher's particular basal series. As we pointed out in Chapter 11, the programmatic philosophies of the various basal series do vary. However, whether it be the Merrill linguistic readers or the Scott-Foresman meaning-oriented, post-look-say psycholinguistic compatible series, the various teaching approaches do not vary extensively.

The basic mix of oral and silent reading, the ability grouping orientation, and the use of supplementary workbook-like material in a carefully graded sequence set the guidelines for classroom practice. Great emphasis is put on the use of the teachers' editions, which carefully guide the teaching process, especially for those teachers who are new at their craft or who wish to be on the safe side.

The reality is that use of the sequential materials, given any of the middle-of-the-road basal series, will successfully guide the normal child from readiness, kindergarten, first grade through mediated reading (phonics/word identification), through third grade, into reading for meaning (fluent reading). Much depends on the wisdom, independence, and imagination of the teacher to make the most of the basal series, invest the reading with excitement and system. No method of teaching reading is entirely teacher-proof. However, as with all human challenges in education, differences are endemic. The artist/educator here knows how to distinguish the problems needing specialized diagnosis and treatment from those whose uniqueness requires flexibility in the pedagogical application of the reading program.

Individualization

We have alluded to the problem of individualized reading programs earlier in this chapter. What with the normal variation in a public school classroom, it takes either heroically endowed teachers with a plethora of reading and language arts materials or extremely able and independent readers to pull off such programs.

Since the process of learning to read brings the child through several developmental stages, which while varying somewhat from child to child in time and pacing are similar for all children in general character, one would here argue against the need for radical individualization through the second grade. Perhaps by third grade, with each child (in a select group) reading fluently, the teacher, armed with a rich variety of materials, could utilize an individualized approach. The sheer number of children in each public school classroom militates against adopting this method as a general practice.

There is a hidden bias here also. Certainly the phonics/ linguistic approach in its various realizations, because it argues for the need to acquire a repertoire of sight/sound correlations, calls for no individualization. Even the early stages of the whole-word/look-say approach, because it had vocabulary sight-word lists, required a strictly controlled vocabulary in those first several grades. One could not reasonably argue for an individualized reading program while requiring the first and second graders to learn to identify a set and basic number of words out of which comprehension would be stimulated.

Thus, one comes to the conclusion that as a teaching method, individualized reading may have some usefulness in a purely literary reading program (non-subject matter such as social studies, science) where the students are relatively independent. Since a great deal of the school program involves interactive discussion—often subject matter studied by the class as a whole—individualized reading has to shrink to a relatively modest portion of the classroom day. This would make the effort-to-impact ratio for the teacher rather low in that the teacher would be putting enormous efforts into a relatively limited portion of the curricular day. What energy would the teacher have left for the subject matters that occasionally need to be taught to the class as a whole?

Language Experience

Teachers who look upon themselves as trend-setters and progressive see *language experience* as a step beyond the rigidities of the basal routine. Similar to the broad embrace of basal texts, *language experience* is useful for all reading philosophies and programs and at all stages in the reading progression. As a matter of fact, an independent energetic teacher using basals can incorporate *language experience* into the sequence of reading lessons.

Most of the basals attempt to get on the *language experience* bandwagon by building into the teachers' edition all the components that have come to be associated with this approach. In fact, those teachers who built their programs on an I.T.A. base including a compatible readiness component have long argued that *language experience* reading instruction can begin in kindergarten at the latest. This is because in I.T.A., since the only symbols that the children need to learn have a one-to-one correlation with the sounds of language (phonemes), the children can begin to write quite sophisticated stories at the same time they are learning to read. They can also read each others' works. This is a total language immersion. It does away with the frustration of misspellings that take place with traditional orthography, where their spoken vocabularies vastly exceed their reading and writing skills.

Experienced teachers, however, can early build into the reading program this same involvement of the child with his or her own life and thoughts without depending on the Dicks and Janes of the basal texts. This is the supposed great advantage of *language experience*. Much of the extrinsic motivation of reading or writing about other people is here substituted with a vocabulary, even invented spellings, that emerges from each child's personal world. Children are here taught to become far braver and more adventurous in their writing and speaking, far more involved in reading and listening when the world upon which their language training is focused is their own.

Again, one can say that whatever the virtues of even supplementing traditional basal reading materials with a *language experience* element in the curriculum, *language experience* can be used with all scientifically and philosophically diverse programs. In fact, its concentration on using all the facets of the language skills that we need to learn renders *language experience* acceptable to all current creeds in reading, given a student population that can benefit from the element of independence that *language experience* requires.

It is important to remember that *language experience* is not a reading program or a curriculum. *Language experience* includes no philosophical interpretation as to what reading is. Nor is there an interpretation or a position as to how children actually learn to read, except in the sense that reading constitutes only one element in the language experience of the child and should not be separated from writing, speaking, and listening with a critical and creative mind.

Systematic Instruction

As our population has increased over the past fifty years, the reading levels have declined, especially since the end of World War II in 1945. Part of the recent dip in academic performance in reading can be laid to the confusion, if not chaos, in reading education in the past twenty-five to thirty years. The substitution for look-say/sight methods by phonics, while it may have rescued a small percentage of non-readers, has crippled many more.

Probably the greatest disaster can be laid at the door of the counterculture movement in education which mirrored events in the outside world. The demographics of the time provide one clue to the problem—many millions of young-sters coming of age at a time of great affluence. "Do away with the grim academics of the Cold War 50's," they cried. "Stop oppressing the young; liberate us all!" Their names are now a faint memory of an educational nightmare.

Many children became the victims of this perverseness, all in the name of freedom from the imposition of the adult will. The confusion of disdain with bureaucratic administration and school organization (often warranted) with the traditional teacher-guided disciplines of study wreaked educational havoc from which our society is still reeling. It is a cause of the qualitative slide that we have experienced in the late 1970's and early 80's.

If there is one methodological maxim that has to be reinstated in the teaching of reading and the other language arts, it is that mastery does not just happen. It must be sweated for—by the teacher and by the children. This does not mean that it requries senseless drudgery. Not at all. Children must become their own greatest motivators to work and to learn. This is the art of the master teacher.

It is not that the teacher manipulates the children to want to exert themselves. The search for knowledge and mas-tery is self-motivating, self-satisfying, its own greatest reward. However, it cannot be achieved through a five-hour "bull session" in a classroom. This is too often the way of a lazy and incompetent teacher, one who refuses to do the hard work of teaching.

Reading and the language arts, the reader will recall, are symbolic tools, part of that middle integrational array of skills that we use to mine our inner intellectual potential. The intelligence is there, just waiting to be released. A child cannot sharpen his/her intelligence in the world of written communication by watching television or glancing at a book's pictures. For a child, it is half a lifetime's careful and gradual study, under the supervision and guidance of teachers who will not allow the casual laziness of even the brightest child to slip by.

This is why one of the criteria of a reading program's full realization is the time set aside each day for careful instruction and critiquing in the classroom. Comprehension of reading materials, carefully checked, creative ideas stimulated to reveal themselves in written and oral forms, papers corrected, redone, all the nitty-gritty that creates the building blocks for intellectual power. As in all things important, it takes work to achieve success. The good fortune for the teacher is that this work should be fun for the young. It means learning to concentrate, to apply one's mind to a potentially tricky task. Good teaching method demands that the teacher, whether within the individualized classroom structure or with basals, demonstrate to the child both the need and the satisfaction of completing an important task well.

Family and Home

For so many years in education, the whispered truth among the professionals was when it comes to things like reading or math instruction, keep the parents out. They might foul up whatever the teachers are attempting to achieve. It was an era when the fit between well-meaning, eager parents and professionally-trained teachers and their programs was less than glove-like. That was a time when parents were generally less educated than were the teachers. It was also a time when parents had greater expectations of schooling. The still naive family would send its children into an institution it believed was on the advancing wave of modernity.

Now, parents are often not merely better educated than the teachers, but have far more wherewithal to travel with their children, expose them to widely educational and broadening cultural experiences. The school today, by contrast, is often dis-educative in the sense of providing a philistine and cold institutional environment. In truth, an educator can no longer say with justice to the parent "stay out of the educational nest, you may foul it."

Further, it is more than fair to say that education takes place primarily in the home. The values and attitudes of the child toward all learning are shaped in the home. If the parents do not read, if they keep the television on constantly, are not interested in the performing arts, world events, are themselves without discipline in their professional and personal lives, the children will pick up all of this.

I would argue strongly that the school and the home should be a seamless continuum of learning. The close mesh between what the school is attempting to achieve and what can be maintained and buttressed at home has always been essential. In their rush to solidify their professional credentials, educators have missed this crucial relationship. As a matter of fact, the schools have been and still are the butt for the educational failures of the home.

How can one fairly judge the success of the school reading program for children if the parents do not read to them, do not talk to them about their books and writings, and to stimulate them to great enthusiasm and effort. Many homes today are barbaric settings where learning and culture are absent. Even if we downplay the genetic correlations of intelligence, we cannot expect much from schooling for children of such backgrounds. It is essential for the profession of teaching to cry out loud and clear, "Parents and community, if you want your children to prosper in their schooling, if you want them to read, write, and compute, then *you* had better provide a base upon which the school can build."

The teaching profession must make the family and the community its allies and ask them to continue to further the concrete curricular work of the classroom. The result would be a unity of effort, which I believe would not denigrate the status of teacher. Rather it would dignify it in its role as part of the community of educational leaders.

FURTHER READINGS

Bereiter, C. and S. Engelmann. (1969) *Distar.* Chicago: Science Research Associates.

Bettelheim, B. and K. Zelan. (1982) *On Learning to read.* New York: Vintage Books.

Hansen, J. and P. D. Pearson. (1983) "An instructional study: Improving the inferential comprehension of good and poor fourth grade readers." *Journal of Educational Psychology.* Vol. 75, 6, 821-829.

Kamil, M. L., ed. (1981) *Directions in reading: Research and instruction.* Washington, D.C.: National Reading Conference.

Pearson, P. D. (1982) "Asking questions about stories." *Ginn Occasional Papers,* #15. Columbus, Ohio: Ginn and Co.

Peterson, B., ed. (1985) *Convergences: Essays on reading, writing, and literacy.* Urbana, Ill: National Council of Teachers of English.

Stauffer, R. G. (1980) *The language experience approach to the teaching of reading,* 2nd ed. New York: Harper & Row.

Veatch, J. (1978) *Reading in the elementary school,* 2nd ed. New York: John Wiley.

13

The Talents of Children

One or Many

I T IS CLEAR that language ability is not the one and only in the sweepstakes of intellectual development and success. What our new knowledge has shown us is that language and its ancillary performance modes—speaking, listening, reading, writing—are vehicles for human intelligence. They are important, of course, and especially at the end of the twentieth century, literary skills are the key to using one's intelligence efficiently and productively.

However, it would be erroneous to argue that persons of high intelligence, yet who have language handicaps, sometimes lacking even a basic education, cannot flourish, to a find a niche in a world that cries out for productive, creative forms of thought. It is simply not valid to view language function as synonymous with intelligence. Remember, the first hint of future reading success is a child's number ability. This tells us much about the nature of human beings' peculiar intelligence.

We must first distinguish between surface- and deep-structure skills. Naturally, at this stage in our progress, our knowledge of the human mind is so suffused with controversy and conjecture that we speak with no more than metaphorical surety. At least the majority of scholars see a general factor of intelligence being in some way modified by specific skills that reflect mysterious individual talents. Whether these talents are simply skills that are developed by education or training or are indeed preternatural talents gained with intelligence we cannot yet know.

In one way of looking at it, we could see that an Einstein or a Stravinsky could have exchanged places. Their productive genius was a power of mind that depended on education, on cultural and family background. It could have been channeled into various professional expressions. Could the military leader have been an equally enterprising business executive, could a great philosopher have been equally successful as an explorer into unknown geographical realms? Such conjectures merely reveal to us the importance of the varied talents or genius of human beings. Without the differences, we could not have had the richness that characterizes great civilizations.

In our own time, even on occasion with a look back into history, we note individuals of various talents and skills—Plato, philosopher and poet; Cicero, poet and statesman; John Locke, medical doctor and philosopher; Bela Bartok, composer and performer; or take Leonardo! Certainly significant achievement in any domain cannot be achieved without general competency in life and behavior. Thus it is probable that all those individuals who gave evidence of great performance talents or special creative insights have in addition that special intelligence and power that define all gifted human beings.

Yet, and here I would like to persuade the reader, there are many highly intelligent people, the graduates of the best collegiate institutions, who show no special genius, no highly developed creative performance thrust. Some show extremely high I.Q.'s, high verbal and math S.A.T.'s, but remain generalists, extremely good at what they do—as doctors, businesspeople, professors, civil servants.

There have been examples in this day of the mass media of individuals with enormous memories—verbal or mathematical—or significant talents for drawing or for playing musical instruments. Sometimes they are precocious youths, sometimes individuals who carry on in the world at modest jobs, raise families. They have one faculty that is developed to an extraordinary degree. In certain cases, they are mentally retarded—"idiots savants." Having merely one unique ability without the skills to generalize it in life is a mystery that does not fit into any recognizable model of intelligence presently developed.

We do know that the loss of faculties, whether through external wound or stroke, often results in the loss of discrete abilities and functions. It is thus possible that in an "idiot savant," such an area of the brain has been subjected to an extraordinary development without the concomitant richness and breadth of brain development that characterize the high I.Q., the "g" (general intelligence) of psychometrics. At any rate, the existence of these variations in the character and make-up of intelligence in humans does lead us to assume two levels: one a deeper, perhaps even unspecialized, area of intellectual possibility, what we call at various times deep structure, cognition, competency; and the other more mid- or surface-structure performance levels.

The great philosopher uses language differently than the great poet. They are both writers using their literary sensibilities with deep understanding and creativity. Can we judge one to be of higher intelligence or of more protean creativity than the other? Hardly. They seem to have roughly equal deep-structure, but quite different performance realizations of this intelligence. Could their performance skills have been interchanged through differences of backgrounds and education? Perhaps.

The Spelling Lesson

The teacher of reading is but one of a number of educational specialists, each setting forth the priority skills that the young must develop. While of special importance, the reading and language arts program is still but one dimension of the educational process. This process must always be viewed as primary in the sense that we want to develop a general competency in the child to mine whatever special talents or performance skills the child has and thus insure his/her long-term social, personal, professional growth.

These preliminary remarks are made to introduce a concept of instruction and general educational development that must encompass, and indeed transcend, the reading program. The material to be offered here derives from what we have learned about spelling and about grammatical and syntactical skills. The latter categories are relevant but to a lesser extent. It is spelling ability that has turned out to be the *bete noire* of the language program, as the new psycholinguistic interpretation has revealed it.

At one time, spelling skills, like penmanship skills before them, were held as essential signs of an educated person's development. Poor spelling indeed gave the individual poor marks in our calculus of the educable. Woe to one who did not shape up in spelling, more difficult to get into Harvard than a rich man into heaven!

Now we are a bit wiser. Penmanship we see as a sensory/motor skill that some have and some have not (to the point of *dysgraphia*), but which constitutes a minor learning disability, usually unrelated to other language skills. With enough persistence, this individual will learn to type. If the disability extends to typing skills, then an added effort is called for. A vault into executive status brings the wherewithal to hire a good secretary with good shorthand skills and typing facility.

Spelling too is a function of what we call surface-structure—integrational skills that harmonize both the visual and the auditory modalities. Most naturally poor spellers can be taught to keep a dictionary at their fingertips and check every other word. At some point, the natural spelling sense (which involves visual memory engrams) will be displaced by more conscious intellectual solutions. The individual learns to spell by invoking another intellectual modality, which allows him/her to spell better, yet not ever with the naturalness that national spelling bee finalists can muster.

Spelling is thus a language skill that does not invoke deep-structure intellectual powers. Rather, spelling ability harmonizes the visual and auditory language pathways of the integrational level of brain function. There are probably dozens of different kinds of spelling difficulties from which people suffer. Thus there is probably no one way of solving the spelling difficulties of the young. Each difficulty has its own special neurological source that issues in an apparently similar result—spelling incompetency.

The teacher's role ought to be to lessen the child's sense of incompetence, to make him (usually a male) understand that his failure here does not reflect on his inner intelligence. Then the challenge is to help him find his own way out of the spelling neurosis, with dictionary, word lists, whatever works. Most important is the rule, don't make a capital case out of small failures of surface-structure abilities. They are not crucial and they often mask powerful deep-structure abilities and talents that could be manifested in other areas of performance.

What spelling tells us is that many skills are relatively independent of the deeper intellectual reality of a child's potential. A good teacher and a wise school system study these matters carefully in each child, for, often, the reality is substantially different from what outward appearances seem to show. Too often, we are bowled over by the superficial tinsel-like glitter of facile skills, whether spelling, computation, oral reading, or beautiful penmanship.

What we should be looking at more carefully is the child who has a hard time achieving the norm in these academic performance areas. Behind a child's gnarled efforts may exist a reading vocabulary a bit more advanced than the spoken vocabulary, certain special math concept understandings, even if often marked by mechanical computational errors. The variety of subtle manifestations of this nascent intelligence is legion. What is clear is that it is having a hard time manifesting itself. And why not?

This is an intelligence that will grow and grow. The reading and writing are in fact means toward an end, the clothing of thought in an outfit that can communicate itself powerfully and clearly. That for a large part of the individual's academic career the clothes are ill-fitting, that the socks don't match, is an indication of possible individual creative power. Our role as educators is to find the proper line of clothes (performance skills) that will enhance this special intelligence. Perhaps the child is a future poet or novelist, philosopher or legal scholar. The old words and patterns will never fit this mind, which is *sui generis*. To penalize the child at the very beginning of its journey because it doesn't have the expected superficial performance fluency is to destroy a flower that is simply different from prior models.

"The One Best Thing"

In a recent interview, a well-known and successful violinist who several years earlier had emigrated from the Soviet Union described some of his experiences. He had left behind all his valuables, including a fine violin given to him by the Soviet government for his solo and orchestral career there. "I came to the United States with only two dollars in my pocket and look what I have been able to accomplish in five years. . . ."

An Egyptian engineer, dissatisfied with his life in his home country, emigrated to the United States, worked at menial jobs as he studied English and American engineering theory and practice at night. In eight years, he was head of a multimillion dollar computer software company, an industry that did not exist in Egypt.

In the mid-sixties in the South Bronx of New York City, a principal of a junior high school described his attempts to deal with a situation in which both the schools and the community were literally dissolving. Vandalism practically obliterated school after school; arson and self-destruction gutted the homes and lives of the people. It was nearly the end of the world for the South Bronx, except . . . In one junior high school, the philosophy of the school trumpeted by the principal was "do your one best thing." Every teacher and every student were put on their mark to find in the students' day-to-day school and after-school life that "one best thing" that would make them proud of their achievements and of themselves. That junior high school came through the hell largely unscathed.

What unifies these stories? It is that achievement in some realm of endeavor, an achieved skill, a basic educational orientation, the ability to be outstanding in one dimension of life will have enormous personal and social fall-out that will go far beyond particular skills. In a word, the achievement of a performance skill of value to society is not merely a mindless virtuoso attainment. To do anything of value for your fellow humans, the skill, whether it be music, engineering, or even stickball on the city streets, will touch your deep-structure abilities. One kind of powerful ability revealed to the outer world tends to radiate inward to transform the individual's confidence and awareness, inevitably to affect the skills in other areas of life.

The violinist came to this country not merely with two dollars. He came with a million-dollar education and knowledge, which were quickly transferable. The Egyptian engineer had a deep-structure understanding of his own language, the basic approaches to engineering in theory and practice. He could learn new things quickly because there was already an internal map waiting to be filled in. Stifled talent in one country, given the existence of a deep-structure understanding of principle, could be expanded on in the new surroundings.

The junior high school principal had intuited the truth. Each individual needs to gain access to his best talents and skills. Once these are developed, an internal map of achievement will be created within which the person's intellectual potential can be released. It will undergird and enrich the "one best thing." A sensitive and wise educator will gently coax these uncovered deep-structured abilities in that one special area and try to extend the light of achievement and confidence to the wider spectrum of skills.

Given that an individual has intelligence, a basic competence to deal with abstract relationships, to investigate causes and effects, to create a map out of human experience within which new ideas can be absorbed into a viable structure of understanding, our educational task requires that we release these abilities through a performance skill—reading, writing, speaking, musical performance, visual artistic skills, mathematical ability. As long as we do not try to create mindless virtuosi in any area of schooling, we can expect that individual success in one area of education will have its impact both on the person in becoming a "well put together" individual as well as radiate outward to the other subjects upon which the individual could focus the particular slant of learning that has already earned him/her success in the primary achievement field.

This is particularly true in an area about which we spoke earlier—reading. Joseph Wepman was the first to argue that we ought to eschew remediation in terms of the given school reading method. By searching for the modality of learning suitable for the unique individual having difficulty with the school method, we might find access to deep-structured, fluent patterns of reading. The theme has always been to find the modality for successful learning, no matter what the subject matter might be. Then, after real learning begins to take place, experiments with remediation might be begun to explore the possibility for extending one successful opening to the larger spectrum of subject matter skills.

Language Skills and Schooling

Let us summarize the points made thus far in this chapter and, by implication, the earlier chapters concerning the relationships between schooling and the language arts skills and the wider issue of the individual's learning potential, what we have here called "the talents of children." Some children arrive at school with all learning systems "go." They make easy transitions from readiness to mediated, then to fluent reading. They write and speak well; spelling and penmanship are more than satisfactory. However, these children may not be the most able in terms of long-run potentiality. The key element is the intelligence that is released by these surface-structure abilities.

Another child, having all kinds of difficulties, not merely in spelling, but in processing the grapheme or phoneme relationships into fluent reading, might have great talent. Despite these difficulties, such a child could even develop into an important writer. To an insistent, persistent mind, the langauge blockade might constitute the first challenge for a somewhat handicapped but unique creative personality. Teachers need to look beyond the success or failure of learning skills to the powers of the mind that are attempting to erupt from below.

There are no easy directions for recognizing such talent. What we must do is rely confidently on the intelligence and perceptiveness of the teacher—the most important educational variable. Perhaps it takes a deep-structured, creative intelligence to recognize the dawning abilities of another able mind?

Significance of Reading Problems

In our educational outlook, we have strongly emphasized verbal ability and, of course, today, ability to work with language is often the prelude to other high level performance possibilities. That is why reading and language skill failures are so traumatic to child, family, and school. Yet it should be constantly reiterated that as important as it is as a medium for scholastic, then professional success, reading ability constitutes only a surface/integrational means for accessing the deeper competencies that lie below. We simply do not understand why it is that so many dyslectics and learning-disabled individuals have high intellectual abilities. Is it that the complex neurological wiring of highly intelligent individuals more often tends to get scrambled? [See Appendix]

Though the educational process of unscrambling may be difficult and not without trauma, when revealed, the intellectual processing potential remains powerful. So it becomes worth our while not merely to assist the fluent virtuosi in reading, but also those who might have powerful access modalities elsewhere. Recall Ludwig van Beethoven's increasing deafness. Then recall the growing involvement with his inner map of the musical world. It was a completely deaf composer who produced the late quartets, piano sonatas, and the Ninth Symphony.

With Beethoven we have a good, though not unique, example of a supreme genius, out of touch with the apparent world of sense experience, fluencies, the variety of human and social modalities—bereft of family, hearing, even intimate love. It was he who plunged deep into the arcane, unheard symbolism of musical composition. As we read Beethoven's notebooks, we can see his struggle to express his ideas through the notation. The scribbled notation seems almost a barrier to his thought. Yet without the notes, the ideas would remain unembodied. Thus he has to work them out, scrawls, scratches, obliterations and all.

The problematic reader has the same difficulties, struggling with letter and word identification, scratches on paper for handwriting, and spelling that misses more often than not. To some teachers, such a person is an academic failure. For the insightful teacher, other signs are more important. Intelligence will have its way. If the child is not crushed by a failure in reading or general language arts, these abilities may shine elsewhere, even, in time, in language use.

Varied Intelligence

The most widely accepted view of the nature of intelligence is that in its broadest power to comprehend abstract relationships there is an underlying unitary essence that we call "g." Humans are not made up of separate unattached skills—virtuosi-like idiots savants. Further we expect that some of us are destined to be highly intelligent generalists. Others, equally intelligent, may develop a special vision or ability in some area of great social importance. The charismatic military leader not only must charm his soldiers, raise their morale and willingness to perdure under conditions of sacrifice. He must also be a strategist and tactician, able to organize large groups of men, equipment, plan for supply lines. A great general cannot merely cry out "Charge!" Much intelligence has to go into organizing the operation before the ultimate moment of engagement. This is a special quality of high intelligence.

Here is our educational challenge. We need to balance in our educational planning the variety of ways intelligence shows itself, not to ignore the generalized achiever, also not be overwhelmed by the great virtuoso, to help the student realize the wider potentialities of this specially powerful intelligence. It is a long road from entrance into kindergarten to entrance into graduate school. During this time, the fate of highly variable intelligences and talents will be in the hands of the school, the teacher, and the family—quite a daunting responsibility.

Deep Structure and Success

The educational rationale for a pedagogical and curricular approach to "the one best thing" is that in finding out what a child does best, we can show him/her the intellectual potential in that activity, whether it be math or swimming. Every human activity meriting social recognition requires thought, discipline, training, and plain old savvy. By breaking through an activity's purely surface skills to the deeper level of principle or theory, we can awaken in the students' minds the reality and existence of this deep-structural level. Once aware that success in the "easy" area opens up the possibility for using this power of thought in other areas of life, we have the potential for creating a truly educated person.

Our philosophy is that the full utilization of a person's "g," or intelligence, depends upon a penetration through the superficial skills—which most students are content to utilize if the teaching allows—to the deeper potential. It is fair to say that these higher abstractive powers mature late. The formal thought level of the Piagetian model of intelligence begins toward the end of the junior high school age. Thus it is necessary that the school allow as many academic options as possible to remain open until puberty begins to release those torrents of energy. Then, the full nature of a person's individual talents will begin to show itself.

FURTHER READINGS

Gardner, Howard. (1984) *Frames of Mind.* New York: Basic Books.

Horn, J. L. (1976) "Human abilities: A review of research and theory in the early 1970's." *Annual Review of Psychology.* Vol. 27, 437-485.

Itzkoff, S. W. (1983) *The form of man: The evolutionary origins of human intelligence.* Ashfield, MA: Paideia Publishers.

Keating, D. P., ed. (1976) *Intellectual talent: Research and development.* Baltimore: Johns Hopkins University Press.

Laycock, F. (1979) *Gifted Children.* Glenview, Ill.: Scott-Foresman and Company.

Oden, M. H. (1968) "The fulfillment of the promise: Forty-year follow-up of the Terman gifted group." *Genetic Psychology Monographs*. Vol. 77, 3-93.

Piaget, J. (1973) *To understand is to invent: The future of education*. New York: Grossman.

Vernon, P. E. et al. (1977) *The psychology and education of gifted children*. London: Methuen.

14

Universal Literacy?

Politics

T OO OFTEN THE issue of literacy becomes entangled in politics. We live in a world where universal solutions seem good. Everyone must be the same; dissidents make us nervous. The schools are the natural butt of our failed dreams of educational utopia. Why can't teachers get every child to read? Why the astounding rate of functional illiteracy which in an advanced nation such as ours should not climb into the percentile teens, possibly even above?

Is such a universal ideal truly desirable in a vast intercontinental society such as ours? Would the reasonable outcome of the enormous efforts that would be required for attaining a better literacy rate be worth the effort? These are fair questions. Literacy is often considered to be the ability to comprehend fourth grade reading material. Most urban newspapers are written with a fourth grade vocabulary and syntactic structure. What great social advantage might we accrue as a nation to have boosted all of our adult second and third grade readers to a level of fourth grade?

A philosopher once made the claim that universal literacy is not the panacea in the twentieth century that it was in the nineteenth. In the twentieth century, we have taken people out of largely agrarian environments where they had a practical relation with reality and placed them in vast urban metropolises where their world of reality is the make believe of political manipulation and mass media. Do we encourage their sense of self-determination or offer them freedom by educating them to a fourth or fifth grade level so that they can be seduced by the official media of the powers-that-be? Indeed, is a little universal literacy really a good thing?

As in all things that are subject to political rhetoric, the facts tend to become a bit fuzzy. First, that crucial question, what do we get from the attempt to raise the reading competency level to fourth grade level? Will we indeed be proud of a population with the competency to read the local tabloid or a porno magazine? Second, is the lack of literacy—or even high reading competency—a result of our educational system? Is it remediable by insisting that schools and teachers create literate citizens regardless of the facts at hand? Then, do we hold only the teachers responsible for the results?

Third, don't we have to factor into the literacy equation those many millions of people who are of retarded intelligence who cannot read much beyond a primary grade level of comprehension? Certainly, to admit such a fact in our egalitarian and universalistic climate of political opinion is distasteful. Nevertheless, the evidence is clear, a large percentage of our population lies below the 85 to 90 I.Q. minimum level of reading and writing educability.

Fourth, there is another population that numbers in the unknown millions. This group has at least average, often well above average intelligence. These individuals are the clinically reading-disabled. We are still in the dark ages when it comes to knowing how to help these persons read on a level equal to their intelligence. The mere wanting to help them read well will not achieve it in the immediate future. On the contrary, there is good argument for helping these individuals find uses for their perfectly useful intellectual abilities in other vocations or areas of life.

In general the truism holds in reading as well as elsewhere: before we take action, we must understand what the facts are and what ratio of success to effort we can expect to achieve. On the basis of all the evidence available to the medical, scientific, and educational communities in mid-1980's United States of America, the solution to our literacy problems seems to lie in a different direction than the popular media would have it.

The Long-Term Problem

The proper long-term social question with regard to reading and literacy must be based on a rational assessment of our situation. Virtually no one disagrees that the widening of the educational net has led to a watering down of average educational achievement and literacy. We see this most vividly in the opening of access to a college level education for a large proportion of our population compared to early twentieth century percentages.

As a result, a bachelor's degree means much less than it did before. This is not merely because it no longer has elite status. The S.A.T. scores have declined for over a generation. There are colleges giving out degrees today whose standards of achievement are probably less than that of an ordinary high school diploma of the 1930's. Finally, look at the best seller lists. What is the reading public itself purchasing?

The evidence cannot help but dismay an impartial student of the problem.

The result is what in kindness can be called cultural decline. It is an uneven decline, since relatively large numbers of our populace still read worthwhile books, periodicals, and newspapers. They enjoy the fine arts and in general give vigorous support to the best in the social and cultural scene.

On the other side of the picture, social competency and cultural interests match the dismal literacy levels. Remember, it was not so long ago when large groups of relatively uneducated and virtually illiterate Americans were deeply interested in high culture and education. It was these people who helped to raise our nation to its leadership position.

The two cultures that live side by side in the United States today, however, reflect a discomfiting socioeconomic picture. Yes, there are those whose skills in language and the other symbolic tools of the educated now allow the parlaying of these educational achievements into high economic advantage. One cannot argue that able, educated, literate people in the United States now have no socioeconomic opportunities. One is hard put also, to make a factual case for the unavailability of educational opportunity because of economic or social discrimination. The truly isolated individual is rare today. The blockages are more subtle. They lie rooted in family, in traditions of deprivation and dependency. They need more radical solutions than merely availability or exposure to education.

Another aspect of our uneven achievements, educational, economic, and social, lies in the misguided laissez faire attitude of the representatives of high culture and even government with regard to our social, cultural, and educational ambience. The concentration on personal enjoyment, the lack of concern with cultural standards, the toleration of ever lower standards in our mass media places a heavy burden of choice on those individuals who could go one way or the other.

The turn away from individual and family responsibility is at the root of the high incidence of illiteracy. The school and the overworked, overabused classroom teacher are not at fault. If parents allow the T.V. to blare forth all hours during the day or night, children will not learn to read or think. The two processes, seeing and hearing a T.V., as against reading and thinking about the words on paper, operate through different intellectual systems. In the long run, competency in difficult and challenging professions needs the thinking skills that reading and writing develop. T.V. watching will never be the answer even given the higher cultural levels of the Public Broadcasting System.

In short, millions of citizens could be lifted to a higher level of literacy and therefore technological and vocational competency—leave aside become conscious of high culture—by a concentrated social and educational effort. This is one area in which we could achieve truly significant material progress without miring ourselves in the unknown complexities of turning illiterates into readers of low-level literary materials.

Social and Educational Improvement

It needs reiteration: education does not take place primarily in the classroom. The home and society at large are the environments where human beings are shaped—in their maturation, values, attitudes, desires. If we want to improve our national levels of literacy, both to raise the quality of our culture as well as to undergird the economic revolution presently underway, we must use the school as an educational stepping stone that will lead from the home to the larger community.

We cannot raise standards in the school unless we convince parents that serious changes in family life are necessary to improve the intellectual and cultural quality of experience for the child at home. The television sets must be clicked off, books, newspapers purchased and read, and the life of mindless amusement altered to include a higher intellectual intake.

At the same time, the powers-that-be in the legislative and executive departments of government must be persuaded that while freedom of expression is guaranteed under the Constitution, there is little in the media that is in reality *un*regulated. Just as we supervise water supplies, increasingly monitor air quality, there is no reason why government cannot put its efforts into encouraging better T.V., radio, periodicals. Instead of protecting ever lower common denominator standards through the First Amendment, we might try to elevate the general tone of human expression.

The Hellenic Greeks made this kind of cultural goal their overwhelming passion. The state itself supported and encouraged the theater, civic festivals of high cultural tone, and indeed put enormous resources into building visually and emotionally powerful environments, such as their "high city" (Acropolis), in Athens and elsewhere in Greece.

Reading with understanding and judgment is not acquired quickly or easily. Like all skills, especially abstract intellectual ones, critical reading demands practice, work, and always the mental aspiration to read ever more challenging material with good comprehension. There are not enough hours in the school day for this. Thus, before we go off blaming the school and the teachers for our declining literacy levels, let us first examine the literary tone in our society. What do we offer our citizens? Second, let us educate those parents that need to be so taught that it is their behavior with regard to newspapers, magazines, or television that will determine their children's attitudes. Parenting has never been easy. Its rewards come from the long-term commitment.

Increasing Our Knowledge of the Problem

Another difficult but potentially important reading issue needs study. We accept the fact that there is a large percentage of children with specific reading disabilities. The fact that the percentages vary so greatly relative to the school problem is usually due to the net by which we include children in this category. We obtain a larger percentage of children by including those with seemingly marginal reading problems, those that often do not fit into the clear-cut slots for dyslexia.

Some factual evidence thus hints at the possibility that a larger proportion of our population than we would like to admit reads at lower levels than their individual and optimum intellectual abilities would indicate. Too many children read below their indicated intellectual levels.

Today our knowledge allows us to understand why this may be the case. As we have pointed out, reading is but one means of intellectual expression, of which there are many others. Reading, as important a skills as it is, lies in the integrational area of the brain, yet in touch with the deeper semantic world of intellectual potential. It takes many years of study to mine those potential intellectual skills through reading and writing. Our variable abilities in the language skill areas argue that different approaches can be made in schooling over the long term to hone our language abilities to bring them closer to our intellectual potential.

Contrast this with the rapidity with which mathematics and chess wonders can access this intellectual potential, often rising to the top of their fields in their early twenties. In the field of language, only poets show such precocity. Philosophers, historians, great novelists often need many years of maturity and discipline to climb to their peak.

The educational question is, how may we take into account the enormous variability in language skills that exists in our nation? What kind of testing and diagnostic techniques can we develop to reveal the underachieving reader and writer? Then, what are the programs that would bring the language user of great potential to his/her peak? We have not until recently understood the reading process as being primarily an integrational level skill, only one among others that accesses deep-structure intelligence and brings it to the surface in a variety of instrumentally useful abilities.

An intriguing part of this problem is uncovered by a comparison of ourselves as a people with the Japanese. There is much talk today of the Japanese population having on the whole a higher I.Q. than exists in the United States population. There are the obvious differences to be accounted for, of course. We have a much larger and richer turf than the Japanese. They have many more people to the square mile. The Japanese are certainly more ethnically and racially homogeneous a people and have lived longer with severity and deprivation than we have.

On the other hand, some argue that at the top of the intellectual/creativity spectrum the Japanese cannot compete with our most creative innovators. They are excellent at copying and systematizing knowledge and applying it in a disciplined practical manner. This suggests that Japanese intellectual potential might be highly condensed, a so-called smaller standard of deviation in I.Q. While they may have on the average a higher ability, their highs on average may not be as high as ours, nor their lows as low. (Their I.Q. curve rises and descends more precipitously.)

In the area of reading, these facts invite interest and some support. Where reading difficulties in Japan surface, they seem to show up more evenly at the bottom of their intellectual scales, slow learners = slow readers. On the other hand, the Japanese show an amazing lack of the traditional kinds of reading disabilities that plague us. In some studies on this topic, the blame is placed on our baffling orthography (spelling system). One of the several orthographies that Japanese children must learn is Kana, a phonetically highly regular alphabet. However, considering the variety of American reading disabilities and the theoretical unlikeliness of a simple phonetically regular alphabet solving our own reading dilemmas, this "solution" raises puzzling questions. Further, the Japanese do learn to read with other, different traditional orthographies. Few reading disabilities are here revealed either.

Is our problem due to some unusual brain structural problem that has settled into European and North American populations? Will we find the Chinese and Koreans—ethnically closely related to the Japanese—also free by and large from the kinds of reading disabilities that we have? These are still open questions that need study and research.

What is indicated in the above discussion is that the new psycholinguistic perspective on reading that I have attempted to set forth in this book, while it may resolve some old conundrums, does raise new issues and problems. This is as it should be. We will always be challenged to study and learn about what is important to our individual and national destinies. It is critical that we go armed intellectually and educationally to fight *tomorrow's* wars against ignorance, not *yesterday's*.

FURTHER READINGS

Chall, J. S. and C. Snow, et al. (1982) *Families and Literacy.* Final Report of the National Institute of Education. Washington, D.C.: U. S. Department of Education.

Jaeger, W. (1945) *Paideia: The ideals of Greek culture.* 3 vols. New York: Oxford University Press.

National Comission on Excellence in Education. (1983) *A nation at risk: The imperatives of educational reform.* Washington, D.C.: U. S. Department of Education.

Weber, G. (1971) *Inner-city children can be taught to read: Four successful schools.* Washington, D.C.: Council for Basic Education.

APPENDIX

Explaining the Reading/ Integrational System

We have earlier identified three dimensions of the human reading system. There are both neurological brain structures as well as dynamic learning processes in the sequence of learning to read. Each of the three seems to vary from each other and from person to person, in strength, power, and rate of development.

1. The sensory/perceptual systems—the eyes, ears, touch, and to a much lesser extent smell and taste—give us the information from the outside world (external experience) that provides us with the first materials out of which learning takes place. Without this first level of "knowledge," language learning—speaking, listening, reading, and writing—is to an extent immediately impeded. Reconsidering the plight of the

profoundly deaf infant will bring home this fact. Of all the senses, hearing is the most crucial for language learning and then for reading. As we have pointed out in Chapter 10, a little bit of residual (naturally occurring) hearing goes a long way to allow the other two reading systems to develop and function.

Let us momentarily skip to 3. This is the final and in many ways the most important aspect of the reading system—intelligence. As practically every commentator on reading has noted, and as is especially emphasized in the Federal Government's 1985 report, "Becoming a Nation of Readers," the ability to extract implications, unstated relationships, causes and effects from the written paragraph is a key to a good and often profound reader. The words on the page themselves only give us a hint of the meaning Their relationship to each other is vital. It is on the context of reading material that our intelligence has to concentrate. In the early stages of reading—kindergarten, first, second grade, most children have a functioning natural linguistic (spoken, auditory) intelligence that runs far beyond the books that they are learning to read. This intelligence is invariably adequate to the contextual demands of the reading process. Given that all reading systems are "go," we see differences in intelligence making their mark from about third grade on, when the faster, deeper-thinking child pulls away in reading from his less able compatriots.

Now let us focus on number 2, the connector between sensory/perceptual input and intellectual grasp or understanding. There is a reason that we put forward a distinct "integration/reading" system. After about a century of study with regard to language skills, especially reading, we have found that we were mistaken in considering only two variables in this process, (a), the sensory equipment the child brings to bear on the written letter or word, and (b), the intellectual system that eventually will determine the depth of understanding.

Explaining the Reading/Integrational System

Recall for a moment the experiments done in the 1950's with so-called Kohler lenses in which the perceptual world was turned upside down. After a few days of wearing these lenses, the subjects found that somehow in the perceptual/brain system, a compensation took place so that the world once more "looked" right side up. These lenses, however, were not compensated for by the brain when it came to reading. The reading material always remained upside down, even while the world was now right side up.

These experiments merely reinforced what kindergarten and first grade teachers have always known. A child's skills in the perceptual world—identifying objects, faces, or even pictures on paper—do not predict how the child will fare with abstract symbols—letters or words on paper. The human mind seems to be split already into skills of ordinary recognition—auditory and visual—and the differing skills of letter and word recognition. That differences also exist between an individual's ability in mathematical symbol skills and verbal symbol skills is well recognized by psychologists and educators. (Note the two S.A.T. exams, math and verbal given to high school seniors.) Yet even here we do not fully understand the nature of the brain systems that seem to distinguish high intelligence in either or both math and language skills.

We can conclude from this evidence that looking at the concrete perceptual world outside ourselves is different from looking at reading material. To understand the meaning of the objects in each realm, seemingly different aspects of our sensory/perceptual and brain systems seem to be involved. This is one of the reasons that educators plead with parents: "Looking at television, even good television, may increase a child's understanding of the outside world and allow him/her to speak more intelligently about it. However, it will not help the child to extract information and meaning out of written material. Only actual reading and writing will accomplish that. This necessitates as much practice, carefully prepared and sequentially skilled, as one develops in the ordinary perceptual world. A couple of hours a week of reading and writing will not do it."

So already we have a mystery about the relationship of the sensory/perceptual system, intelligence and reading. Some mighty able people who see/hear perfectly and function intellectually and professionally superiorly are not good readers and/or writers. Why?

Let us first proceed to accumulate a bit more data in describing the peculiar thing that we call the integration/reading system. Every experienced teacher will probably be able to recount amazing and often sad but amusing tales about certain of their young charges whom educators describe as "word-callers." These are children, normal in every other sensory/perceptual respect, who learn to "read." Not really.

For, these children can decode the written material to sound. When asked to read orally, they are young virtuosi, except that they usually read with odd oral expression. When asked to read silently, and then questioned about the reading material for meaning, they are at a loss.

These children exemplify what linguistic scholars used to describe mistakenly as readers. The children decoded the written, visual marks to their auditory/spoken language equivalents. However, we do not consider this to be reading. Reading is really the extraction of *meaning* from the written material. One does not have to vocalize or subvocalize the material to understand it. (See Chapter 9, "Fluent Reading".) Children that educators call word-callers can decode, but they can't read, for their abilities to find meaning are barred by an intellectual problem of one sort or another. One can note here that (1) the sensory/perceptual system is fine; (2) the integrational/reading system is operable, but (3) the intellectual system seems not to be functioning.

By contrast, there is that mass of individuals whom we call reading-disabled. These are not the lazy, malinstructed, culturally handicapped, intellectually slow, nor the deaf or the blind. These millions of children see and hear normally when tested with the sounds and objects of the ordinary world. When tested in their intelligent behavior and understanding of the outside world and when tested with other kinds of symbolic materials, such as mathematics or musical notation, they prove to be highly able. In fact the history books are littered with the names of great people of real intellectual accomplishment from Leonardo da Vinci to Winston Churchill who had difficulties in some aspect of language learning and performance.

What is even more bizarre is that these so-called "dyslectics" suffer from an extremely wide variety of specific language disabilities, from handwriting, spelling, syntactic problems to difficulties with certain grammatical categories of writing. Sometimes it is almost as if each reading-disabled person comes to our attention with a slightly different and thus unique language learning problem.

It is clear from all of our experiences with such individuals, who are often males, that something specific to their neurological/brain structure is fouled up. Neither their sensory/perceptual input skills nor their deep-structured intellectual abilities are impaired. As Joseph Wepman noted, something somewhere between sensory input and final intellectual absorption of the knowledge has become crossed. Often this short-circuiting process can be outgrown and the individual learns to read and write well.

For others, the road to intellectually powerful language performance is not as smooth. They never completely overcome their disabilities but must learn to use other modalities to get the information into the intellect from the sensory/perceptual system. And they often do. We have heard bizarre stories of individuals who have passed themselves off as medical doctors, sometimes surgeons, never having been able to get into medical school because they were reading-disabled or their academic records were poor. But being highly intelligent, they have been able to perform well enough, accessing their knowledge from other sources. Eventually, a little thing like not being able to read a notice or a sign betrays them and they are exposed.

As we can see, here too is an area of human performance that cannot be explained by invoking the workings either of the sensory/perceptual systems or the intellect. An example of the problem of channeling diverse sensory inputs into a common intellectual understanding follows: consider the spoken words "four," "fore," "for." To demonstrate the concepts, we could raise four fingers, write the number "4," or pound the table: knock, knock, knock, knock. There are individuals who would have difficulty organizing this so-called cross-modal information to utilize it properly. Somehow some of these inputs have been malperceived or misunderstood. Simply, it could be a classic integrational failure. The wiring in the brain was short-circuited.

It need not be in reading alone. Learning disabilities extend to tone deafness, math and number blindness, left/right body recognition, and a host of delicate functions that in one person or another is slightly askew—and the fault is not in the actual reception of information through the sense organs, nor in the intellectual functions, but rather in the processing and integration of this information in the relevant parts of the brain.

We know, for example, that the language areas can be found in at least three parts of the brain (Broca's—left frontal; Wernicke's—left temporal/parietal; and the midbrain hemisphere-connective areas). We also know that the associated cortical areas around these language structures seem to be specialized in function: frontal lobes—will power; temporal/parietal—reasoning. Thus what we here call the integrational system of functioning is broader than the purely language functions of which reading is a crucial part. Here too individual variability can be traced to differing neurological patterns. Certainly the actual variable reading skills with which each of us is endowed are part of the wider integrational set of human functions.

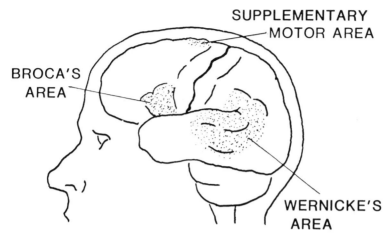

Figure 13   Speech Areas of the Brain
The three speech areas of the left hemisphere of the cerebral cortex. They seem to have separate functions—Broca's area: vocabulary, inflection, syntax; Wernicke's: understanding, meaning; supplementary motor area: articulation. How these natural speech areas of language interrelate with reading and writing is unclear. Certainly the integration of visual and auditory inputs as they relate to the meaning structure of experience already acquired by the child is crucial. Messages must be relayed to and from each of the speech areas for total linguistic capability to be fulfilled.

Another way of understanding this peculiar relationship of reading/language skills with the broader functions of intelligence is to note how these functions have evolved in the human line over the past millions of years. Chimpanzees and other apes and monkeys certainly do vocalize, but their screeches and hoots emanate from a brain-controlled vocalic structure that is subcortical. This means that the vocal expression of subhuman anthropoids is controlled by the limbic system, or the midbrain, which expanded to prominence among the mammals in general.

Human spoken language, however, is centered in the areas of the neocortex, the evolutionary advanced or reason-

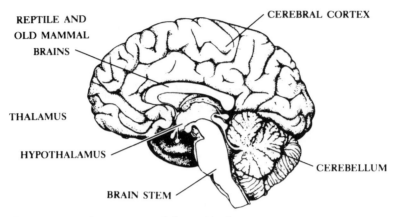

REPTILE AND
OLD MAMMAL
BRAINS

CEREBRAL CORTEX

THALAMUS

HYPOTHALAMUS

CEREBELLUM

BRAIN STEM

Figure 14   Language and Brain Evolution

Humans probably had a rudimentary form of language centered in the left cerebral cortex several millions of years ago. While spoken language is natural for all members of the human race, written language came into use but recently. To facilitate reading and writing, the brain must utilize complex circuitry that calls into play not merely the new brain, the cerebral cortex, but the old auditory and visual processing areas of the basic mammalian brain as well as the allocortical connections, which link up both ancient and recent structures, Many quite subtle processes can go askew from the moment of conception (genetic factors) through gestation and birth (congenital traumas). Even in our life development, small injuries to the skull can cause losses in various language functions (listening, speaking, reading, writing).

ing parts of the brain. When by chance the language areas of the human cortex are badly damaged or need to be excised, all human vocal abilities disappear except certain primitive guttural expressions, remnants of our ancient vocalic past still controlled and directed by the limbic or old mammalian areas of the brain.

Even though the language areas are distinct from other parts of the brain, the evolution of human intelligence probably saw an intimate and reciprocal growth of cortical intelligence and language function. Yet it is odd that so-called "word-callers" have such an excellently functioning reading/oral skill, but so little comprehension. In many respects, they remind one of the idiots savants, who can achieve wizard-like skills in verbal memory, computation, musical or artistic performance, but who understand little of what they (they are mostly male) are achieving, and are not able to extend this one skill to other, broader performance attributes.

In all the conjecture about the actual locus of the so-called integration skills, and what and where things go wrong when an individual reveals such a disability, one set of relationships seems to emerge. This is the peculiar bicameral structure of the human brain. We have a left and right hemisphere, connected by a tightly-wound 3/4-inch knot of fibers called the corpus callosum which makes the human brain unique.

How this affects the language skills of each individual is both fascinating and mysterious. The left hemisphere seems to be specialized for language, sequential, logical, and intellectual behavior. The right hemisphere is the holistic or perceptually-oriented hemisphere. While there is some evidence for language facility in this hemisphere, it is rudimentary. In addition, the lower brain seems to be more intimately wired to the right hemisphere and thus there is an emotional (affect) quality to the responses that emanate from the right side of the brain.

Samuel Orton, in the 1920's, noticed a correlation between learning-disabled children and their lack of clear lateralization dominance (right- or left-handedness). He then urged teachers to delay reading and writing instruction until the child showed a clear preference, arguing that the immaturity of the nervous system in some children caused this lateralization delay. Until they were clearly left- or right-handed, they would have language-learning difficulties.

Years after, it was realized that lateral dominance was shaped by the controlling hemisphere. Thus right-handers almost always had their language areas in the left hemisphere.

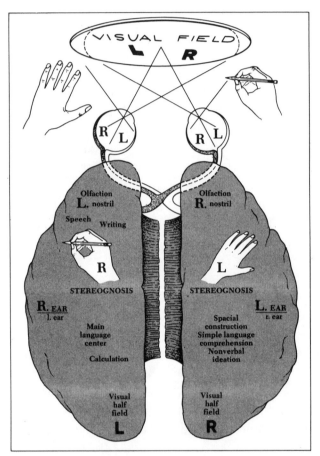

Figure 15   The Two Hemispheres

In this schematic diagram, the left and right hemispheres are separated by a "severed" corpus callosum (a bundle of two hundred million neural fibres) that ordinarily transmits information between the hemispheres. The fact that both auditory and visual information are projected into the opposite hemisphere of the sensory organ that they enter constitutes part of the problem in integrating language information. Because linguistic function is not so easily shunted to the opposite hemisphere, there is more room for dysfunctional processing. Each of us has a different combination of specialized learning functions located in each hemisphere. Much of the variability in language skill development can be attributed to the unique "split brain" structure of *Homo sapiens*.

228

Left-handers were somewhat divided, with most having their language areas in the right hemispheres, but some in the left. It became clear too that a disproportionate percentage of the left-handers of good intelligence had learning problems. It became clear also that much of the so-called integrational disabilities arose from problems associated with the lateralization of the brain, a process controlled by an as yet unknown complex of genes.

In addition we do know now that lateralization is present even prenatally, but that often there are injuries to the delicate brain at birth and in the neonate, sometimes even prenatally. When this occurs there is often a shift to other parts of the brain of these skills of lateral dominance. Many left-handers are created as part of the development of neurological compensation in the child. Since a large majority of the learning-disabled are males, and there is a strong hereditary component (given the evidence), the genetic element cannot be overrated.

Norman Geschwind has done research that seems to draw a correlation between precocious and brilliant young mathematicians and left-handedness, myopia, auto-immune difficulties (allergies, asthma), and migraine. Somewhere in all of this is the reality that aberrations in the organizations of the brain, either genetic in origin or as part of a series of minute neurological environmentally-induced events, affect the relationship in the operation of both hemispheres in processing information, linguistic, and other.

These relationships must be somewhat independent of the perceptual/sensory intake of information and the deeper, slower, long-term organization of this information that is part of the total neuronic structure of the cortex, our general intelligence. Because these factors of processing information seem to operate independently of the other two dimensions, we can argue tentatively that they need to be studied as a discrete element in the reading process.

We do know that dyslexia is often an inherited problem, as it can be traced through the generations in certain families. However, the causes, as we have noted, are not always congenital in origin. Things happened to children and adults in their lifetimes unassociated with their biological destiny, and these problems reveal themselves as typical characteristics of integrational defects.

Naturally, the average child of, let us say 90 to 110 I.Q., who sees and hears, reads and writes, thinks and performs, would never reveal to us that these three elements of our learning equipment are separable in function and in scientific analysis. It is the special case that reveals the existence of variable structures of the brain and thus variable performance by individuals.

The sum of all of this is that teachers and parents must keep these facts in mind. The process of reading comes about through a unity of diverse biopsychological structures in the human nervous system. The integrational system is a crucial element in attaining reading competency. It must be recognized and borne in mind. That indeed, is only the beginning of the problem. Then come diagnostics, motivation, pedagogy, curricular materials, and a real learning environment, in school, home, and society.

Index

They Wrote on Clay, Edward Chiera, Fig. 1, 27.
Torrey, Jane, 75.
Truk Islanders, 23.
Tunnel vision, 115, 118.

U

Uncertainty, reduction of, 98-100.
Understanding Reading, Frank Smith, 16, 47, 74.
University of Chicago, 43, 111; School of Education, 65.
Upper Paleolithic peoples, 25-28.

V

Ventris, Michael, 29.
Verbal Behavior, B. F. Skinner, 53.
Visual skills, 23-24, 82-83; peripheral vision, 117; *see* Tunnel vision.

W

Walcutt, Charles, 54, 125-126, 160, 162; Fig. 8, 164-165.
War, Cold, 42-43.
Washburn, Carleton, 65.
Watson, John, 53.
Weddel, Klaus, 71.
Wepman, Joseph, 48, 111, 115, 146, 172, 176, 203.
Wernicke's area, 224; Fig. 13, 225.
Whole-word method, *see* Look-say.
Why Johnny Can't Read, Rudolf Flesch, 43.
Winnetka, Illinois, 65.
Wood, Evelyn, 115.
Words in Color, 169.
Writing: alphabetic, 17, 84-86, 88; chronometric marking, 25-26; logography, 17, 31, 59, 85-86, 216-217, *see also* Japanese; origins, 26-28; pictographs, 27-28; syllabic, 29-30.
Wundt, Wilhelm, 39.